How to Bury a Goldfish

and Other Ceremonies & Celebrations for Everyday Life

Virginia Lang and Louise Nayer

Skinner House Books
Boston

Cover design by Kathryn Sky-Peck, Text design by Suzanne Morgan
Printed in the United States

ISBN 1-55896-519-X
978-1-55896-519-5

09 08 07
5 4 3 2 1

Library of Congress Cataloging-in-Publication Data

Lang, Virginia E.
  How to bury a goldfish : and other ceremonies and celebrations for everyday life / Virginia E. Lang and Louise B. Nayer.
        p. cm.
  ISBN-13: 978-1-55896-519-5 (pbk. : alk. paper)
  ISBN-10: 1-55896-519-X (pbk. : alk. paper) 1. Family—United States.
2. Family recreation—United States. I. Nayer, Louise. II. Title.

HQ535.L343 2007
306.87—dc22

                              2007005546

We gratefully acknowledge permission to use the following materials:

Excerpt from "First Song," from *What a Kingdom It Was* by Galway Kinnell. Copyright © 1960, renewed 1988 by Galway Kinnell. Reprinted by permission of Houghton Mifflin Company. All rights reserved.

"Song of the Barren Orange Tree" by Federico Garcia Lorca. Translated by W.S. Merwin, from *The Selected Poems of Federico Garcia Lorca*, copyright © 1955 by New Directions Publishing Corp. Reprinted by permission of New Directions Publishing Corp.

"The Worm's Waking," from *The Essential Rumi: Translations by Coleman Barks, with John Moyne*. Reprinted by permission of Coleman Barks.

Anonymous poem beginning "She opens her window . . . ," translated by Tin-Yum Lau. Reprinted by permission of Tin-Yum Lau.

"Old Song," from *The Collected Poems of Robert Creeley, 1945-1975* by Robert Creeley, © 1982 by The Regents of the University of California. Published by the University of California Press. Reprinted by permission of the University of California Press.

"Wail Sighting Off Kehoe Beach" by James McColley Eilers. Reprinted by permission of James McColley Eilers.

"Each of us is an artist . . . " by Arthur Graham. Reprinted by permission of Betty Graham.

"Bedtime Prayer Thoughts" from the *UU Kids' Book* by Charlene Brotman, Barbara Marshfield, and Ann Fields. Reprinted with permission of Charlene Brotman.

Prayer by Gary Kowalski reprinted with permission of the author.

Excerpt from "That Love May Grow" from *Prairie Smoke: Writings from the Heartland* by Melinda Morris Perrin. Reprinted with permission of the author.

Excerpt from "A Theology Adequate for the Night" from *Instructions in Joy* by Nancy Shaffer. Reprinted with permission of the author.

Dedicated to Aunt Margaret, whose unwavering belief in my worth was a constant inspiration and support; to my husband, Dean, whose love and encouragement sustains me in my work and my vision; to my stepdaughter, Heather, for her insight and support; to my daughter, YuWen, who is the light of my life and a constant reminder of what is good and true; to my new daughter, Zoe Berman; and to my mother, who always wished she had the words for things. —V.L.

Dedicated to my husband, Jim, whose unselfish love guides me and frees me; to my daughters, Sarah and Laura, daughters of my soul; in memory of my father, Herman Nayer, who taught me compassion and to love learning; and to my mother, Dorothy Nayer, who taught me courage and to finish what I started. This is also dedicated to all my family and friends, young and old, for your belief in my writing and for your love. —L.N.

Contents

Beginnings

Fabulous Firsts

Red-Letter Days

Transitions

Loss

Holidays

Introduction

The sun rises, an enormous ball of fire thousands of miles wide, yet we hardly notice. Alarm clocks buzz unmercifully in our dark rooms and, as if on automatic pilot, we do our morning duties, alone or with family, only subliminally aware of the magic that has just occurred. The sun has risen once again and the darkness has vanished, but we have not been a part of it.

How can we see the magic in each day and connect with the natural world, our fellow humans, ourselves?

When many people are struggling simply to survive, we are constantly bombarded with hollow materialism; stores stay open seven days a week, beckoning us, and demands of work and family far exceed our ability to respond. In our hearts, we know that something is missing, that we are not fully present in our own lives, that the carousel of busyness and consumerism is spinning faster and faster, placing in jeopardy the very earth on which we live. We have traded lighted candles and soft shadows for the neon glare of computer screens and the bleeps and blips of our techno-logical toys.

We seek a certain numbness to quiet the fears of a post-911 world. We live in a time of terrorism, natural disasters, and the fear of global warming. We are understandably overwhelmed, but this is precisely why we need to be especially vigilant about deepening bonds with family and friends and encouraging hope in all our children.

How, then, can we reclaim the very part of us that makes us human? How can we establish a loving pace amid the rush and chaos?

This book is a guide to noting and celebrating the everyday events of our lives: marking the passage of a girl into womanhood; helping a single friend begin a new home life; taking time to fully mourn the death of a loved one; feeling that it is okay, even right, to simply sit in silence. The nights we light a candle for a loved one who is ill or help a young child celebrate a difficult school decision are nights we cherish and remember, times when we slow down and fill our lives with softness and caring for one another.

We, the authors, met twenty years ago at the Blue Danube Café on Clement Street in San Francisco. Our meeting was coincidental. Ginny started talking to Louise, who was breastfeeding her daughter Sarah and welcomed Ginny's openness. We found out we knew people in common from the East Coast and realized, as we got together more and more often, how much we had in common and how much we both wanted to build a community embracing family and friends, young and old—especially children—in our circle of love.

In time, we came to write this book together, inspired by both our individual journeys and our shared vision. After years of cherished memories—sharing birthdays, job challenges, the deaths of parents, and the many small victories in the lives of children—we decided it was time to write down some of the ceremonies and rituals that had meaning for us, in the hope that others could benefit.

We are not looking to replace ancient truths or the community and faith that can be found in a place of worship, but we have found useful and heartfelt ways to express ritual and ceremony in lives that embrace blended families and differing backgrounds and lifestyles. In addition, we have written and discovered some beautiful words to give voice to the feelings we all experience at poignant times in our lives.

The book's title was inspired by an event common in many households with young children, the death of a pet goldfish. Both of us have befriended and buried small animals, grieved for the loss of elders, celebrated friends' decisions to change careers, and honored the many milestones in children's lives. As with the fish burial, we offer ideas for simple ceremonies—some based on time-honored practices, others completely new—that can be done in a short time and can be easily adapted to any reader's lifestyle.

We have written a "family" book because we believe that we all have family, however we choose to define it. Traditions for singles are included, such as a "shower" for a young man getting his first apartment and an annual celebration for a single person who is special in the life of a family.

We believe our everyday lives deserve celebration. As our world grows more complex, it takes more thought to do less. Through simple ritual and ceremony, we slow down and open our eyes to the beauty and meaning in our lives, awakening to the natural world and the richness of our relationships with others. When we take time to see the sun rise and set, to really see the exploding colors of the universe, we awaken ourselves from cynicism and despair and open our hearts to the mysteries of nature, our bodies, our lives.

This book is an offering. We hope you will accept it as an invitation to take time to fully experience what is most important in life: family, friends, and the many wonders of our everyday lives.

Everyday

In the everyday events of our lives we express who we are. When we rush through our day focused only on our destination, we are not fully alive, not able to see and savor the precious moments that fill our daily lives: letting water cleanse us in the morning, acknowledging coworkers instead of hurriedly racing past to our offices, sitting quietly around a dinner table at twilight, and lighting a candle before each meal. Every day offers us rich opportunities for renewal.

Greeting the Day in Peace

Dawn
rises from darkness.
Birds sing,
invisible,
among the trees.
The sun bathes us to wake.
—Louise Nayer

Getting up and out in the morning is often a purple haze of activity—gulps of coffee, toast on the run, and hastily blown kisses while scrambling to find the book bag, the keys, the homework, and the briefcase. It seems the day has legs and is already running away before it even begins. It takes determination and ritual to take back the morning. Even if you hate mornings and can't function until your second cup of coffee, easing into morning may help you center yourself and reclaim your day.

What You Need

- A Zen chime (available at many department stores) or a clock radio
- An uplifting photo of someone you love or a special painting

What You Do

There are many gentle alarm clocks now available; some offer sounds of nature, others vibrate you awake. Try waking to the quiet and calm of a Zen chime that slowly pings in intervals that gradually shorten. Or simply get a clock radio and set it to a classical or soothing music station. Once awake, turn it off and let your eyes rest on a photo or painting you love, hung in your direct line of vision. Then take a simple body inventory while still in bed. Notice the sensation in your ankles, your legs, and so on, until you have slowly climbed up your body to your head.

Then take a minute to reflect on your current situation and the demands of the day, picturing yourself moving smoothly and easily from task to task.

Finally, think about the people you most love and focus on their whereabouts and well-being this day. Picture your safe return home after a satisfying day.

Calling Your Body from Sleep

> *It is morning.*
> *You are called from sleep*
> *By the song of the sun.*
> *Plant your feet on solid ground;*
> *Reach up your arms*
> *To the blue ceiling of sky.*
> —Louise Nayer

The first moments of our day set the tone for the rest of it. When we leap out of bed to the sound of an alarm clock and rush to shower and dress, we are abusing our bodies instead of honoring them in a spirit of gratitude. Our bodies support us in everything we do, yet we often ignore them and take them for granted.

The theologian Matthew Fox speaks of awakening our spiritual and physical energy through chakra work. The chakras are important intersections in the body where energy is especially concentrated. There are seven master chakras in the body, each with its own distinct function. The ritual that follows is an attempt to make contact with each of these powerful junctions in our bodies and to evoke, in a conscious way, their full potential. In Eastern thought, this is like inviting the uncoiled serpent that lies sleeping at the base of our spines to gloriously unwind.

What You Need

- Five minutes in bed
- A meditation for the chakras

What You Do

Place both hands at the appropriate chakra and invite yourself to be present in the day with these words:

A Meditation for the Chakras

Base of your spine   *May I be grounded in the deepest pulse of the earth, connected to the source of all life.*

Lower abdomen (just below your navel)   *May I live with passion and commitment this day.*

Solar plexus (just below your heart)   *May I be powerful, bringing purpose and direction to all I do.*

Heart   *May my heart expand with compassion toward others.*

Throat   *May I speak my truth.*

Forehead   *May I bring my fullest knowing and creativity to life.*

Top of your head   *May I praise the good work of others.*

When you have finished, put your feet on the ground and take three deep breaths, picturing yourself moving easily and gracefully, bringing your best to your day.

Morning Shower

The water is as clear and simple
as the inside of a prayer.
—Eugene Ruggles

Water is used in many rituals throughout the world. It is a symbol of purity and cleansing; in baptism it signifies new life and renewal. We can embrace this feeling of renewal every time we step into the shower or bath, if we take just a minute to let in the wonder of water.

What You Need

- A shower or bathtub
- A natural sponge

What You Do

As you shower, luxuriate in the incredible gift of water. Our bodies are mostly water; our planet is covered in water; water and sunshine make it possible for plants to thrive. Fill your sponge to saturation. Then, squeeze it over your head, letting the water run down your face and arms—take in its warmth, its refreshment, its silky sensation as the water purifies all troubles from the previous day and night. Repeat this until you are ready to emerge from your shower completely fresh and renewed.

The Family Morning Sendoff

To each other, we were as normal and nice as the smell of bread. We were just a family.

—John Irving

YuWen's father is a very big man. One of the things he likes to do first thing in the morning is smother YuWen and me in his big arms in a "family sandwich." At first I'd be the pastrami, he'd be the cheese, and YuWen would be the pickle. Then, each new day, we'd all pick new identities. Over time, we have evolved into a sundae (more appealing to a four-year-old) and we change flavors and toppings each day.

Funny little rituals take on the importance this one has for us because, in this small gesture each day, we demonstrate to YuWen that we are a family and that she is an equal player in this family. I know that as a petite only child living with two much older, much bigger people, she must find it hard to remember that she has a distinct place and is a key "ingredient." It's also just a lot of fun to do! —V.L.

What You Need

- About one minute before leaving the house
- A place to gather

What You Do

Just before leaving the house in the morning, say, "Time for the family sandwich." Have each person pick an ingredient that suits him that day. Some days are pastrami, some are cold turkey. Let each person pick what he wants, no matter how crazy the sandwich gets—we've had marshmallows-with-liverwurst days! Then squeeze the sandwich together in a huge hug and have everybody take a bite (kiss).

A Workplace Check-In

I wish I loved the human race;
I wish I loved its silly face;
I wish I liked the way it walks;
I wish I liked the way it talks;
And when I'm introduced to one
I wish I thought, What jolly fun!
—Sir Walter Raleigh

I am not a morning person. When someone tries to talk to me before I've had my coffee, they are met with a half-hearted groan. My husband, on the other hand, is painfully cheerful the minute his eyes open. After twenty years, he still talks to me in the morning as if I were listening.

When I worked in a hospital, many meetings were held early to accommodate physicians' schedules. I hated these sessions and missed most of what was said.

Whether you work in an office, a school, or a bakery, you start the day or night with human beings, in all their quirks and splendors. Some come to work charged up with ideas and enthusiasm; others come in angry from some household grumble; still others are just not awake. To make the day productive and pleasant, we need to recognize one another's individuality and offer a measure of compassion to those who may be troubled in some way. —V.L.

What You Need

- Ten minutes
- A place to meet as a group

What You Do

Ask your work group to sit around a table, preferably in a circle, for a ten minute check-in. Have each person take one to two minutes to acknowledge the group and to convey any big news in his or her life. It may be a personal anecdote, such as "My cat ran away last night and my children are very upset," or a simple expression of gratitude to be back with the group after a vacation or illness. If you have a rambler in your group, you may need to appoint one person each morning to call time at the two-minute maximum. Gently remind the group of Shakespeare's adage, "Brevity is the soul of wit."

After each person speaks, the group should say together, "May we offer our best to one another this day." Though it takes just a few minutes, this practice invites everyone to be present, to feel heard, and to remember that they are important in the lives of their coworkers.

Writing as Ritual Time

In this secret room
breathe in lavender,
lilac, rose;
breathe in the voices
of those who have gone before.
Let their stories
skim the waves
like elegant birds.

—Louise Nayer

Everyone is a writer. Whether you write for a living or for pleasure, every one of us can benefit from taking the time to put thoughts and feelings on paper. I have written many exhaustive imaginary letters that helped me to clarify a feeling or resolve a relationship. Though they were seldom sent, they helped me to move forward and, later, to remember what I was feeling at a particular time.

Julia Cameron, in her beautiful book *The Artist's Way,* suggests starting each day with three "morning pages," just to get engaged. I take this idea one step further and say to myself, "Just write three bad pages, so I can lighten up and not take myself so seriously." Give yourself the permission to be uninspired and to simply write. You may find that the simple joy of self-expression is a useful way to begin each day, no matter where it leads. —V.L.

What You Need

- A half-hour each morning
- Good tea or coffee in a mug only for you
- A journal
- A pen

- *Perchance to Dream: A Lullaby Album for Children and Adults* by Carol Rosenberger

What You Do

If you go to an office each day, arrive a half-hour before work begins. If you are at home, get the kids off, eat breakfast, turn on the answering machine, and go to the quietest place in your home with your tea or coffee. Take out your journal and pen, sit down, and write. If you have trouble getting started, you may find it helpful to write to someone—a friend, a boss, someone not living, someone you admire or are angry with. Play . . . *Perchance to Dream* or another soothing recording.

Write three journal pages without lifting your pen from your paper. Avoid judgment and do not edit what you write. If you want to rewrite something you are proud of and want to develop it further, do so at another time. This practice is for self-expression only. Over the months, this can become a wonderful ritual of deep connection and self-care.

Meditation for a Child

Then river waves are calmed.
—Li Ch'i

My daughter Laura once said that adults often don't realize that children carry a lot of stress. For starters, schools assign much more homework than they did years ago. Competitive sports, which used to start in high school, now begin in the first grade. Today, many children have less time to dream, for many reasons—they are overscheduled, both parents are working, or the streets don't feel safe—and parents respond to those reasons by finding programs to keep their children occupied.

Even though my schedule allowed me to pick up Laura after school every day, and she could come home and rest, she still felt stress from school and soccer.

At age eleven, she developed exercise-induced asthma after joining a traveling soccer team. We decided to see a Chinese doctor, Dr. Rong Rong Zheng, recommended to us for her expertise in treating asthma. What helped Laura the most in her treatment, I believe, was the meditation she learned.

After going to Dr. Zheng, Laura said, "Soon, I had learned how to meditate. This relaxation cleared my mind. My brain was finally breathing, finally resting." The meditation helped Laura immeasurably with her asthma and her homework. Children who have a yoga or medical meditation practice complete their homework in much less time and retain more. Most importantly, they are relaxed and their bodies are better able to deal with overload. —L.N.

What You Need

- Time alone, twice a day—once in the morning and once in the afternoon or evening before doing homework

What You Do

Go into a quiet room and close the door. Do not turn on any music or the TV. Sit cross-legged and, if you can, place your ankles on the opposite knees, yoga-style.

Lace your fingers together with your thumbs touching, creating a circle of energy throughout your body. Put your hands at the bottom of your stomach, near your bellybutton.

Breathe deeply, using your stomach rather than your chest. Say the number one in your mind. Continue until you reach the number fifty (or beyond, if you wish). Feel the oxygen flowing through your body; think of nothing else but your breathing. If your mind wanders, you say "so" on the inhalation and "hum" on the exhalation to give your mind something to do.

When you are finished, sit with your hands still laced together and your thumbs touching. Starting from your bellybutton, rub your clasped hands in a circle against your body, up to the top of your chest and back down. Do that ten times, breathing deeply as you do it.

The Word Hat

Words are, of course, the most powerful drug used by mankind.

—Rudyard Kipling

Leaving our homes is an important transition, but one we seldom notice. We leave behind the safe and secure dwellings that house our special people and special belongings for a world that brings chaos and challenge along with opportunity. Much of what happens to us is a result of how we prepare to meet the world and what we see in the thousands of stimuli we encounter in an average day. Words can be a powerful reminder that we attract what we think about.

What You Need

- Index cards on which you have written words expressing qualities such as hope, perseverance, generosity, grace, forgiveness, clarity, and so on
- A hat with a flat bottom

What You Do

Place the index cards in a hat. Keep the "word hat" by the front door. Once a week, let each person select one word from the hat to take along for the day. Later, at dinner, have each person share the word he got and how it showed up during the day. For example, a child who got the word *forgiveness* may see that the grudge she is holding against a friend is festering with each day that they do not speak to each other. Generosity may inspire a new thought about a homeless person asking for money.

If there is no shared meal or natural opportunity to share thoughts, each person may choose to write a paragraph about his word in a journal.

Cooking with Children

Long before institutionalized religion came along with temples and churches, there was an unquestioned recognition that what goes on in the kitchen is "holy."
—*The New Laurel's Kitchen*

Fermenting dough, churning butter to cream, caramelizing sugar—these are examples of kitchen alchemy, transformations that remind us of a larger hand at work. When I am cooking with YuWen, watching her little hands discover all the properties of flour or joyfully cover her mouth in chocolate, I am reminded that cooking with children is one of the most satisfying rites of our lives. Being with her and all the beautiful shapes, tastes, and textures of the living things we eat to nurture ourselves takes me to a magical place where time recedes and sensuality triumphs. —V.L.

What You Need

- Time to cook
- Lots of fresh seasonal ingredients
- Willing children

What You Do

One evening a month, plan a family cooking night when the entire family will prepare the meal. Select a menu with fresh seasonal fruits and vegetables. Think about easy jobs to match the age and experience level of each of your children. Be sure to invite and include elders to prepare and share this meal. Ask the children to set and decorate the table with festive, seasonal colors.

Guide your children to use their hands, simple tools, and their instincts when cooking. Notice and talk about the sounds of chopping, stirring, and peeling; look at the rich textures and colors; savor the smells.

Some foods lend themselves well to this type of hands-on event. Among them are corn on the cob, skewered summer vegetables, salads, fruit mixes, and baked goods. Let your imagination roam.

First Fruits of the Season

To everything there is a season, and a time to every purpose under the heaven.

—Ecclesiastes 3:1

Once I had a Swiss cooking teacher who said, "If you have to ask me for the recipe, you don't understand. A real cook goes to the market, sees what is fresh and delightful, and celebrates the sensuality of each trip."

In our world of tasteless winter tomatoes, anemic strawberries, and limp lettuce, markets (or, rather, supermarkets) are hardly sensual wonderlands. They are more like packaging museums dedicated to carefully concealing each item's flavor and texture behind layers of colorful plastic and cardboard.

Yes, we can now get peaches in winter and asparagus in July, but we have lost the sense of the special, the thrill of seeing blood-red strawberries come to market in June, full of flavor; summer tomatoes that smell like the earth itself; corn so sweet it bursts in your mouth. We want all of it, all of the time, so nothing is special any of the time.

With this in mind, it seems especially fitting to mark the end of a season or the beginning of a new one as especially precious, a moment to savor and celebrate. —V.L.

What You Need

- A harvest calendar for your area (call a local fruit farmer for a reference or ask your state's Department of Food and Agriculture for a "Farmer to Consumer Directory")
- A family calendar
- A free weekend

- A good, complete fruit and vegetable cookbook, such as *The Joy of Cooking*

What You Do

Make it a family ritual to celebrate the first fruits of each season. Refer to the harvest calendar to mark on your family's master calendar when each harvest will be in. Get directions to the farm nearest you that allows you to pick your own fruits and vegetables.

Invite another family to go along to the farm, and organize a two-family "cook-in" to can tomatoes, bake peach pies, make delicious jellies and jams—whatever the season offers. Follow the guidelines in an excellent cookbook on fruit and vegetable dishes. Plan a celebratory dinner to enjoy the food; at the meal, join hands and say, "Thank you for the bounty of the earth and the abundance of this season."

If you don't like cooking, invite a child or friend to go with you to gather the brilliantly fresh fruit as a seasonal ritual in itself. Be sure to pick too much and share it. Grandmothers who remember "fresh" will be especially pleased with a gift of raspberries or summer tomatoes and can often show you how to handle what you picked.

Here is an example of a harvest calendar, this one for the San Francisco Bay Area, from *Seasonal Expectations* by Katherine Grace Endicott.

Almonds—September and October
Apples—July through October
Apricots—June
Berries—June and July
Cherries—May
Corn—July and August
Figs—September through November
Melons—June through October
Oranges—December through February
Peaches—July and August

Pears—July through October
Plums—July and August
Pumpkins—October
Tomatoes—August through October
Walnuts—October through December

Tuning in to Twilight

Opal mist descends
rounding jagged mountain peaks,
twilight is falling.

—Virginia Lang

In every culture, contemplative silence has ritual importance. In the Jewish tradition, the family sits shivah when a loved one dies, honoring the deceased through shared silence. In Eastern religions, meditation is practiced as a way of going inside to a place of quiet and inner knowing.

In the Andes, the Q'ero Indians sit in meditative silence at twilight, which they call the hour of power. They believe twilight is a particularly powerful time for gaining insights from within, reawakening us to our life's purpose. Observing the subtle change of light as the sun sets is a lesson in seeing, in breathing, and in being. It is nature's nightly light-and-sound show, free of admission, playing to audiences all over the world.

What You Need

- A quiet place to sit outdoors
- A pillow and a blanket

What You Do

Find a comfortable place to sit outside that is facing west. Take a pillow and blanket with you. Watch the colors as the sun slowly sets, naming them in your mind with descriptive words like *crimson, papaya, violet,* and *russet.* Be as creative as possible, really noticing the dimensions of color and naming each subtle shade.

Spend at least ten minutes in total silence, watching the colors of day meld into the inky blue of night. Breathe deeply and let the concerns of the day fall away. Picture yourself taking off the tensions of the day as if you were undressing yourself of each concern one by one until you are lighter and freer. Stay as quiet and still as you can until you are covered in darkness.

The Family Dinner

Where we love is home
home that our feet may leave,
but not our hearts.
  —Oliver Wendell Holmes

Evening is an excellent time to draw the family together and reflect on the experiences each person has had throughout the day. Unfortunately, in many households, it is a time of gobbled food, ringing phones, and the white noise of television in the background.

So, first decide to make the evening meal an occasion—that is, begin with the understanding that when everyone is seated no disturbances will be allowed to intrude. If the ringing of an unanswered phone bothers you, turn the ringer off. If you are accustomed to watching the news, tape it and watch it later in the evening.

What You Need

- A centerpiece candle of any size
- Matches
- Selected readings

What You Do

Buy or make a special family candle just for the table. Ask a family member to light the candle every night at the start of the meal. Join hands and start to squeeze, passing the squeeze from the first squeezer to the person on her right until it comes full circle. You may want to begin with the youngest or eldest member present or with the one whose birthday is nearest. Then, raise the circle of hands and say, "Blessings on the meal!"

Ask, "Is there someone who needs special thoughts tonight?" Then, with hands still joined, send some silent thoughts of support to a person who may be ill or troubled in some way.

One night a week, choose someone to read a short passage he has written or taken from a favorite book as a way to introduce humor, literature, and beautiful words to your family table. Here is a short quip from Mark Twain to get you started: "Cauliflower is nothing but cabbage with a college education."

Setting a Place for Elijah

Loving Spirit,
Be our guest,
Dine with us,
Share our bread,
That our table
Might be blessed
And our souls be fed.
　　　　　—Gary Kowalski

Many religions and cultures celebrate the sharing of meals. In the Jewish tradition of setting a place for Elijah, Elijah is the unseen guest who is always welcome at the family table. He is a reminder that no matter how little we may have, we always have something to share.

What You Need

- A designated night of the week
- An extra place setting

What You Do

Choose a night of the week to set an extra place at the table. Ask a different member of the family to set the extra place each week. Since Elijah is a guest, his place may be a bit special.

When everyone is seated at the table, join hands and say together, "We welcome Elijah to our table. May we always remember there is enough to share."

Once a month, you may wish to invite someone new to your family to share a meal in Elijah's place.

Nighttime Prayer

I wish the rain would help the flowers grow.
I wish a rose for my family.
I wish people would be happy forever.
                                    —*Laura Patten*

When she was small, my daughter Laura wrote this prayer during a bad drought season—hence, the wish for rain! For many nights over the years, she would say this prayer before bed. In its simple way, the prayer said all she wanted to about the earth, her family, and the world.

Unitarian Universalism encourages children to make up their own prayers. One particular bedtime ritual in a book that Laura's congregation gave her when she turned eight helped her at night-time to move into a place of beauty and rest. —L.N.

What You Need

- A made-up prayer
- Bedtime prayer thoughts

What You Do

Help your child make up her own prayer by first looking at these bedtime prayer thoughts. Then, have her recite her prayer each night. After the prayer, she can recite the bedtime prayer thoughts. Talk with her about each prayer thought, or think in silence together.

Bedtime Prayer Thoughts

Think about things you are THANKFUL for today.
Think of something you feel SORRY that you said or did,
    and any way you can make it right.
Think about something you HOPE will happen, and any
    way you can help it to happen.
Think about being in a PLACE of BEAUTY or a FAVORITE
    place where you feel safe and good.
Think about the people you love
and their love for you.
See each person's face in your mind.
Give them a goodnight smile!

—Charlene Brotman, et al.

The Storytelling Stool

*Every day you see a dandelion floating in the sky as big
as a storm.*

—YuWen

I love to tell stories. YuWen and I have a bedtime ritual that I also enjoyed with my stepdaughter Heather. The girls choose a character (either a person or an animal), the name of the character, and where she lives. I take it from there and spin out a tale as fantastic as I like until I hear the heavy breathing of slumber. This has been extremely satisfying for me and very practical as a sleep aid because it allows the story to be told in the dark! When Heather was little, I had a special storytelling stool. Once I sat on it, she settled down and got comfortable for the night.

Reading books out loud is also a wonderful nightly ritual that many families observe. But I have found that live storytelling is especially intimate and creative (no one else has ever heard this story before) and the girls really use their minds trying to give me impossible combinations—like the green elephant named Delicious that lives on Mars. I also learn what's up in their magical minds, whether it's long-necked dinosaurs or purple unicorns. Some nights on the stool have inspired some really magical stories. YuWen's floating-dandelion mind really responds to magic; the more bizarre, the better. —V.L.

What You Need

- Time to tell a good long story
- A storytelling stool
- A character, a name, and a place

What You Do

Take your place on the storytelling stool. Ask your child to start you off by answering these questions: Who is the character? What is her name? Where does she live?

Place no restrictions; just work with what you get, however challenging. Follow the basics of good storytelling: Present a conflict or dilemma for the character, then a moment of crisis, then a resolution. For example, a blue unicorn from Mars lands on earth, can eat only daisies, is near starvation, but is helped by grasshoppers to find a whole field of flowers!

You will get better with time and may come to find this the most creative part of your day. Just be sure something happens in your story. Little children like an exciting plot, particularly one with a moral dilemma like unfairness or injustice, so pose a dilemma for the character and solve it by the end.

You may wish to hand paint or stencil your storytelling stool with the names of some of your memorable characters, adding to it over time. It will be a wonderful souvenir of precious nights together.

Healing from Deep Hurts

Stand still in this stone blade in the red cedar moon,
Listen to the shamans roam through stars.
—Duane Niatum

When I was four years old and my sister, Anne, was six, our parents were critically burned in a gas explosion. It happened while they were lighting a pilot light in the basement of a rented home in Cape Cod, Massachusetts. Anne and I were sleeping upstairs when the accident occurred.

At forty-two, the age at which my mother was burned and my own daughters were four and six, I experienced panic attacks. In an effort to "get a hold of myself," I went to renowned hypnotist Isabel Gilbert, who has used hypnosis with people all over the world. She made a personalized tape for me that I still listen to and treasure.

Toward the end of the tape, she suggests that I imagine myself as an adult going into the burning house, picking up myself as a four-year-old child, and hugging that child close to me. I say, "You are safe, you are healthy" and take her across the street and into a warm house. This simple act has released the tension from my body (and my past) in a miraculous way. It has helped me to literally and figuratively "get a hold of myself." This is just one of many ways that I learned to heal from the trauma of the past. —L.N.

What You Need

- A few minutes during the day
- Your imagination

What You Do

Imagine a tranquil scene in nature where you feel calm and relaxed. When you feel sleepy, see yourself as a small child frightened and alone. Ask the adult—you—to pick up your child body. Hug yourself as a child and say some healing words. For example, "I love you. You are safe and healthy." If you do this every day and before you go to sleep, the child within you will feel loved and you as an adult will feel safer, happier, and healthier.

Another way to heal from the past is to turn any scary image into something beautiful. When scary images cross your mind, immediately turn them into roses, lilacs, or your favorite flower. The mind can hold only one image at a time. Replacing horror with beauty can help in the healing process. Yoga is another effective way to work with a deep hurt from the past.

The Family Meditation

The heart at rest sees a feast in everything.
—Asian-Indian proverb

Whether we call it meditation, contemplation, or prayer, we can all benefit from focused thought. When many people share this focus, the results can be powerful. In his book *Healing Words,* Larry Dossey documents many studies of sick people whose health improved after people, including strangers, prayed for them.

Many peoples of the world recognize that through prayer, dreams, and visions, individuals can touch the hearts and spirits of other human beings, regardless of time and distance. Imagine the power of family members adding love and insight to the equation. Listening through meditation can help children learn to respect their inner lives and develop self-confidence.

What You Need

- A quiet time when all can easily gather
- A comfortable place to sit

What You Do

Pose a challenge or simply ask a question about a concern that the family shares. Is someone ill? Is the family contemplating a move? Are there financial concerns that need solutions? Is there an unresolved conflict between family members?

Ask each person to sit quietly, focusing on the matter for ten minutes in absolute silence. Then, ask each person to speak from the heart, sharing the insights gained. If no insights are forthcoming, continue the meditation that night in sleep and gather again the next day.

When we sit quietly with something, new sources of creativity become available as we learn to look to ourselves for answers.

Balm for a Tired Parent

If you are not good for yourself, how can you be good for others?

—Spanish proverb

Water is wonderfully purifying and feels luxurious without costing much. Once everyone is tucked in and no longer making demands of you, consider taking time for yourself to relax and restore your body before sleep.

What You Need

- Bath salts or bubble bath
- A candle in a beautiful holder
- A loofah
- A plush towel or robe
- Scented body lotion

What You Do

Close the door after telling everyone it's your private time. Fill the tub high and pour in lots of bath salts or bubble bath—more than you need! Then, turn out the lights, light your candle, and watch the flame create rainbow colors in the bubbles.

Take a mental inventory of your day and think of all the people in it. Was there someone who wronged you? Was there an opportunity to help someone out that you declined? Did you say or do something in anger?

If you have a loofah, scrub yourself thoroughly in all the rough places, like the backs of your heels and elbows. With each stroke, name and release your negative feelings. For example, "I feel bad that I didn't offer to pick up my neighbor's child at school. She really needed the help today." Or, "I'm tired of yelling at the kids about leaving the house on time. Tomorrow, I will create a reward for getting it right, instead of screams for getting it wrong!"

As you name each event or feeling and scrub it away, think through and visualize how you would like the next exchange with that person to go. For example, you might offer to pick up your neighbor's child another day this week. Take three deep breaths after each new vision.

Once the negatives are handled, take three more deep breaths and think of the positive things that happened in your day. Should you be proud of an accomplishment? Was it a beautiful day, a holiday? Naming and celebrating the good things in our lives draws more of them to us.

Stay in the tub until you feel finished with this process and can hear yourself breathing deeply. Then, wrap yourself in your favorite towel or robe and sleep well. Self-care helps you to remember that everyone you touch thrives when you do.

Seeding Sweet Dreams

I do not know whether I was then a man dreaming I was a butterfly, or whether I am now a butterfly dreaming I am a man.

—Chuang Tse

The end of the day can be the very best of times if you just take a moment to bring the day to a peaceful close. Rather than fall into bed exhausted, why not choose to get in bed fifteen minutes sooner to give yourself the chance for some really sweet dreams?

What You Need

- Comfortable pajamas
- A candle in a holder
- A glass of water

What You Do

First, put on the softest, friendliest pajamas you own. Sit on the side of the bed with both feet on the ground. Then, light your candle and hold it in your hands.

Look into the flame and let it burn away any difficulties in the day past. Turn your thoughts to the candle's illuminating power and ask that your dreams shed light on any matters of concern to you.

Take a sip of water after you have asked your question. Then blow out the candle and sleep. You may have your answer sooner than you think.

Creating Space

How many things I can do without!
—Socrates

When I prepared my house for sale, I purged, sending boxes and bags to charities, consignment stores, and starving students. The recipients were grateful, and my home has never been more peaceful. I didn't even know I had many of the things I was squirreling away. Lightening up helps us value what we really do love and keeps things moving through our lives. It creates the space for new people and new experiences to come into our lives.

In my new home, I have a ritual: When something new comes in, something old goes out. Even if it's just a magazine, when one comes in, one goes out. When YuWen outgrows a pair of shoes, she and I give them to a friend or donate them to charity before new ones go into the closet. Moving things along keeps us from getting too attached to things that just end up weighing us down, mentally and physically. It frees us from the past and helps us develop more generous hearts. —V.L.

What You Need

- A scheduled day once a quarter
- All family members
- A designated storage area
- Huge garbage bags

What You Do

At the start of each season, organize a purge day. Decide the rooms to be purged and the degree of purging desired. For example, are you going to remove surface clutter or are you really ready to open closets and drawers? Then, agree to ask if anyone else in the family needs or wants an item you are purging. It saves tears later if you can remember that the old sweater from the 1960s that you hate is in style for your teenager.

Think about later use for some of the items. Is there a young adult getting a first apartment? If so, establish a storage area before you begin or you will just rotate things from place to place. If you have used women's business suits, consider giving them to Dress for Success, an organization that outfits low-income women for job interviews.

Evaluate each object to be purged by asking, "Can I live happily without this?" If the answer is yes, take the item and, as you handle it, be aware of the use it had in your life, allowing yourself to feel whatever comes up. Then, when you feel ready, say, "With gratitude, I freely offer this for another's use." Put it in one of three bags—donation to charity, save for a student, or garbage.

A Weekly Family Meeting

That I may hear your words,
Listen to mine.
That I may know your heart,
Speak to mine.

—Melinda Perrin

At my Unitarian Universalist congregation a few years ago, our family learned about the "family meeting," and we have been meeting regularly ever since. When our daughters Sarah and Laura were younger, many of the issues that surfaced had to do with fairness. We had to test all of our peacemaking skills and remember that we were working together for the common good.

Whether you divide up chores, talk about the family budget, or discuss more serious issues, meeting as a family gives voice to both young and old and helps the household run smoothly. —L.N.

What You Need

- A family meeting time once a week
- A family-meeting notebook
- A talking stick carved with the initials of each family member

What You Do

Choose both a secretary and a leader and rotate each week so that eventually each person will do both jobs. Have the secretary date a page of the family-meeting notebook and record the concerns of each person.

Let each person who speaks hold the talking stick, a thick piece of wood carved with the initials of all family members. No one else is to talk except the person holding the stick. When the next person speaks, pass the stick to that person.

The leader should begin by saying what went well over the past week. Maybe the laundry got done on time, the older child cooked a meal, or there was a nice family outing to the park. Next, the leader should talk about what needs improvement—the plants weren't watered, one person did most of the dog walking, or there was too much television over the weekend.

Each person should then voice what went well and also state his concerns. There should be no interruptions. After each person is finished, other family members may comment and come up with solutions. Maybe the job of watering the plants should be given to someone else. Perhaps a chore list needs to be put up on the refrigerator. Perhaps a family outing should be planned for the next week as well.

It is important that this not be a put-down session and that no one person gets blamed. The family needs to be seen as a unit, with each person trying to help the others succeed.

At the end of the meeting, hang the talking stick on the wall in a prominent place for all to see. The new secretary may then read the notes at the next meeting.

Welcoming a Stepchild

When in the paling darkness of the lonely dawn you stretch out your arms for your baby in the bed, I shall say, "Baby is not there!"—Mother, I am going.
—Rabindranath Tagore

For many years, my stepdaughter Heather came to our home every Friday night for the weekend. It meant a complete change of mode for all of us; she left the comfort and routine of her mother's home and we shifted from two working professional people to instant family. I wish I had thought to create a ritual that would have let her know that we were happy to see her and that she belonged with us just as much as she belonged in her mother's home. —V.L.

What You Need

- A fresh flower
- A family symbol
- A good chocolate

What You Do

Just before your stepchild arrives, take time to think about the visit from her perspective. She may feel off center, miss friends, or be sad about leaving the other parent. Place a small flower on her pillow, or, if you have a family symbol or talisman (ours is a snail), put it on her pillow with her favorite chocolate and turn down the bed hotel-style.

Each week, write a note from one or both of you to go along with the flower or symbol. It can be as simple as "We missed you."

If there has been a sadness or a big event in the child's life, let the note reflect your understanding and willingness to talk if she wants to. She may want to keep a scrapbook of the notes or tack them to a bulletin board each week.

The Family Time-Out

All happy families resemble one another, but each unhappy family is unhappy in its own way.
—Leo Tolstoy

Perhaps the happiest families are the ones that approach the challenges of family life with humor. In my family, for example, I am trying to balance the needs of a sixty-year-old man, a menopausal mom, a twelve year old, and a fourteen year old.

In blended families like ours, the varying ages and experience levels of the family members can present huge challenges. We all need time out from the expectations and compromises required in family life, especially in families with independent souls and teens. As my dear friend Ellen likes to say, "Do we have to be joined at the hip to be a good family?" —V.L.

What You Need

- A family free day
- A setup day to make it work

What You Do

Decide on a date that works for everyone. Set guidelines appropriate for your family. For example: Each person is free to get out of bed, eat, drink, dress, nap, talk on the phone, and come and go without any questions asked. If a child misses a class or practice, he must get permission or make it up. If a parent sleeps in, someone else gets breakfast. If a teenager talks on the phone for more than thirty minutes, he must be sure others don't need to use it. Each person cleans up his own mess.

The idea is that, with common decency in mind, each person is free to think of himself first for one full day.

Be sure to think through the necessary setup. Get groceries in the house, lay the soccer shoes by the door, get someone else to drive the carpool, whatever it takes to make the day run smoothly. If there is an elder to care for, consider a respite-care program; many communities now have them.

Later, at a family supper, discuss what worked, what didn't, and what was learned. If this was a good practice, make it a monthly ritual.

Family Stories

Because the tale of how we suffer, how we are delighted, and how we may triumph is never new, it must always be heard. There isn't any other tale to tell; it's the only light we've got in all this darkness.

—James Baldwin

Mary Pipher, author of *Reviving Ophelia,* has done significant work with adolescents about their sense of identity. One of the things she writes about is the necessity of family stories.

Many of us grow up distanced from relatives, or we believe that what happened in the past is not important. But if we are to feel a part of the long thread of humankind, what Uncle Fred did in 1929 or Aunt Katherine saw as a nurse in World War II all contribute to a distinctive family portrait. If these stories are used for enlightenment and told with wisdom, they can draw families together with the ancient art of storytelling. This ritual can also be done with a group of friends who have been together a long time and have many stories to share.

What You Need

- The family gathered together
- A guide for the evening (this can rotate—children can guide as well)
- Pens, crayons, and markers
- A family storybook
- A tape recorder

What You Do

Pick one night each month or each season to be Family Story Night. If you have a fireplace and it's cold, throw on a log. Serve cocoa, tea, or coffee and sit in the living room or around a table. Turn off the lights and light a candle to create a calm atmosphere. In summer you may want to sit under the stars, around a campfire.

The guide should ask each person to tell a personal story about the past, beginning with either the eldest or youngest. The stories may be embellished but should stay true to the events. Young children may recount stories of when they were three or four.

At the end of the evening, the guide may ask everyone to write his story in the family storybook or simply record the evening on tape. The taped voices of a loved grandmother or a special uncle are a treasure, particularly after they have died.

For those who prefer to create a visual memory, include drawings, pictures, or photos in the book.

Expression Night at Home

We are all attached
like tiny red and white carnations
whose stems touch
at the bottom of glass.
　　　　　　　　—Louise Nayer

Growing up in Greenwich Village and later becoming a poet, I have always had a house full of artists and writers. I moved to San Francisco to be part of the poetry community, immersing myself in workshops and readings. Over the past fifteen years, working full-time as an English professor and raising children, I have found myself going to readings less and losing some of that inspired, magical community that gave me so much.

In an attempt to bring more creativity into our lives, my family has started a monthly gathering at our home on Bosworth Street where both seasoned artists and novices can share their work. Everyone is an artist, so no one is turned away! Our art has included sculptures made from lemons and oranges, piano recitals, poetry and prose readings, and a computer calendar art show.

As people become increasingly fatigued from the pressures of work, this regular gathering adds magic to the month. I have been surprised and pleased at how many people ask, "When is the next Bosworth Café Night?" and how excited they get about practicing a piece on the piano or learning a new song to sing. —L.N.

What You Need

- Invitations with dates for the next six months
- Food and drink brought by everyone

What You Do

Send out flyers marked with dates for the next six months. You can make a Café Night logo or an unusual flyer using your street name.

When people arrive, serve the food and drink. Afterward, sit in a circle in the living room. Ask one guest (a different person each time) to bring a poem, a passage from a book, or a song to begin the evening. It can be something written for the occasion or a favorite song or poem.

Then, begin the sharing time. Keep the performances to ten minutes per person so that people will want to return to the next gathering. Encourage one another, whether the person is a first-time poet or a widely published author. This is a time to remember that the creative spirit lives in all of us. End the gathering by holding hands and passing a squeeze, each person focusing on the beauty of what has been presented that night.

Virtual Shopping

I cannot and will not cut my conscience to fit this year's fashions.

—*Lillian Hellman*

When I am bored, I shop. I don't particularly need anything or want anything, I just like to look and touch and handle things. Once I buy something and take it home, it often loses its fascination for me.

Now that I realize this about myself, I go "virtual shopping" now and then. I take YuWen along and we go into a store on a treasure hunt. I ask her what the most special item is, or the most beautiful color, or the oddest-looking thing. We make shopping a looking-and-seeing adventure, and then we leave. If something that I really want sticks in my mind the next day, I go back. I like to think this is teaching my daughter to be able to appreciate things without having to own them. In a world where so many people are still living at subsistence level, do we really need all the trinkets, fashions, and fixes that sweep our culture? —V.L.

What You Need

- A shopping destination
- Someone to go treasure hunting with you

What You Do

As you shop, let yourself see and describe everything that is beautiful to you. What is the most memorable object, dress, lamp? What is the best example of forest green? What objects are perfectly suited to someone else in your life? Make notes for birthday or holiday gifts. Compare your thoughts with the other person; it is fascinating to get a child's perspective or that of a friend who may have excellent taste.

If you are a catalog shopper, circle every item you like in the catalog as if you were going to order it. Then, go back and draw double circles around your favorite two items. Lay the catalog aside; if you wake up the next day truly wanting one of the items for yourself or someone else and you can afford it, then make the call. But you may find you have already had your fun. If you are an internet shopper, have fun filling your shopping cart, but don't give your credit card information.

A Grandchild/Grandparent Day

Look at me, child,
the wrinkles you see
are only a ledger of memories to me.
Look at me, child,
the blue veins you see
are a great flowing river from you back to me.
—Virginia Lang

When I used to visit my aunt Margaret, we would have coffee and lament the hotel-like nature of assisted living. With everything done for her, she came to feel unnecessary in her own life. The bed was made, the meals prepared, and her social life organized. There was simply nothing left for her to do. Gone were the little things that gave life meaning—making her bed the way she liked it, driving a car, baking cookies, squeezing a grape at the grocery, or dusting her beautiful china.

The assumption that most older people want everything done for them is wrong. There is so much loss when an elder gives up a loved home. It is a double blow to give up autonomy, too. Here is a ritual anyone can do for older loved ones who have lost their freedom. —V.L.

What You Need

- An afternoon date once a month
- A car
- A wheelchair or walker, if necessary
- Patience

What You Do

Offer to pick up your grandmother for a tag-along afternoon, just your usual errands and routine. If walking is difficult or impossible for her, go to a grocery that has special carts with rumble seats (many large stores now have them) or take along a wheelchair. As you go up and down the aisles, put oranges and basil, fresh coffee, and other fragrant foods in her hands so she can feel and smell them. Offer to purchase special items she can no longer get in assisted living, like Cocoa Puffs, baby carrots, pink grapefruit, even old favorites like shoelace licorice. Go slowly enough for her to really take in the experience and look at all the new products she's never seen.

Continue on your errands to pick up a child, drop off mail, whatever you ordinarily do, involving her whenever possible. Cook her a dinner from the groceries you bought together, and let her dry dishes sitting down. Make a date to do this once a month, so she knows it's coming up and can look forward to it. You will share memorable days together just being yourselves. Of course this works for grandfathers, too, or any special elder!

The "No Place Special" Day

Life is what happens to you while you're busy making other plans.

—John Lennon

One of the nicest days in my life was one that went haywire. A babysitter cancellation meant a complete change of work plans and YuWen and I were in free fall until I caught myself and decided to just go with the day. We strolled, window-shopped, bought groceries, and read books at the library, just going with the flow. Over root beer floats, she turned to me and said, "Mama, this is the best day of my life."

Instead of my usual preoccupation with time, school, and agendas, I was present and able to just be with her. She got to decide what we did next, and I got to see the world through her magical eyes. Louise told me her mother used to do something like this when she was young. The two of them would get in the car and her mom would say, "Let's get lost." It is important to allow for spontaneity in our competitive culture and to let our children be children. —V.L.

What You Need

- An unplanned day with your child once a month
- An agreement that both of you get to pick what to do

What You Do

Set off on foot or by car without any idea where you're going. Ask your child for ideas on where to go and what to do as the day progresses. Avoid planning anything—just let yourself go. Children seldom get to create their own day from scratch and will love the chance to take the lead without being told that it's time for this or time for that. In our overly programmed world, "no place special" days are golden.

Learning to Look in Nature

This is how a human being can change:
there's a worm addicted to eating
grape leaves.
Suddenly, he wakes up,
call it grace, whatever, something
wakes him, and he's no longer
a worm.
He's the entire vineyard,
and the orchard too, the fruit, the trunks,
a growing wisdom and joy
that doesn't need to devour.

—Rumi

One day, our family went exploring in the tide pools of Morro Bay with our friends the Maruska family. Katy Maruska and YuWen collected shells and rocks, bits of kelp, and driftwood. As they brought their treasures back to the blanket, I began to look closely at the colors, counting at least a dozen different subtle shades of green, from beach-glass jade to deep spinach. The three of us made it a game to keep finding green and presented our "study in green" to Katy's mom, who is a gifted artist.

Afterward, when I thought about that day, I realized how life can become an exercise in how we see. Before that day on the beach, if someone had asked me what color the ocean is, I would not have said "a study in green," the way I would today.

The ability to see and to keep seeing with fresh eyes is critical in a world that seeks to label, define, and limit. Here is a ritual that allows us and our young children to learn to see. —V.L.

What You Need

- An afternoon once a week
- A place in nature (ocean, woods, a local park, or your own yard)

What You Do

Pick a destination and ask your child to go on a hunt with you to make a collection of all the interesting things you can find in nature—feathers in a yard, polished rocks in a riverbed, unusual leaves in a forest, beach glass at the ocean. Lay out your treasures and examine them together, grouping them by color, texture, or size.

Give creative names to all the subtle shades—robin's-egg blue, blood-orange red—respecting each person's unique perception of color. Some days, you may prefer to make it a study in shapes. Each day you do this, take home one souvenir of your study, and label and date it.

The Men's Group

I'm a self-made man, but I think if I had it to do over again, I'd call in others.

—Roland Young

I love to watch boys at play. One of my favorite movies is *Stand By Me,* a high-adventure story full of blood and guts, humor and pathos. The boys encounter a pond of leeches, a runaway train, a dead body, and the meaning of friendship.

My husband laments the absence of simple boyhood joys in his life. In his work in the corporate world, he is typically confronted with men whose competitive outlook prevents true connection. He longs for a place to share his deepest thoughts and feelings with other men but finds few opportunities to do so. —V.L.

What You Need

- A day off from family and work responsibilities
- A small group of male friends
- An exciting place to be together
- A supportive partner

What You Do

Pick an activity your male friends can all do or want to try. Go white-water rafting, climb a mountain, go on a safari—whatever appeals to the group and fits the budget. The goal is to pick something exciting, new, and full of adventure.

Spend at least one full day together. That night, share a meal that all help prepare. Shop, cook, eat, and clean up without any outside help. After dinner, gather by a campfire or fireplace and throw out a topic that concerns everyone present. It might be the fears of new fatherhood, how to handle a strong-willed teenager, how to date after a break-up, or a humorous topic like "What do romantic partners really want?" Agree that everything will be said in confidence, and give everyone a chance to speak without judgment. If this is a good experience make it a monthly ritual.

As the men's group grows and develops, this circle of men can support one another as a "virtual village," providing counsel and support for their sons and daughters as the children reach adolescence.

Beginnings

Seeds in the ground: new forms created that are able to take root. The cry of a new baby, with its planetary eyes and moon-shaped head; the journey of new parents to keep their love for each other alive; hopes that live on the threshold of a first home.

Our lives are filled with beginnings—being brought into the life of a family, beginning life in a new place, or simply beginning the day in a newly conscious way. When we begin something, we have the opportunity to bring awareness to our beliefs and assumptions, to challenge ourselves to be new, different, better.

Beginning a More Creative Life

Only the dreamer can change the dream.
—John Logan

Everyone has creative abilities, but few of us continue to discover and develop our talents as adults. For many years, I worked as a poet-in-residence at senior centers and nursing homes and was constantly amazed by the poems written by people who had never written poetry before in their lives.

One woman who had Alzheimer's disease wrote about her childhood in Chicago, where she danced on polished wooden floors surrounded by full-length mirrors. I felt as though I was with her in that dance studio. I also worked with a woman who had been an accomplished therapist in Europe. She chose to live a creative life in San Francisco, produced two poetry books, and is now a well-known painter in Europe and the United States. She is also blind.

We are all creative, but it often takes the right people and the right moments in our lives to let us create. Between meeting family responsibilities, paying bills, and working, few of us get the chance to explore our creative sides. But art can actually save lives. I have seen it many times in my work with people who have been allowed to express their deepest feelings in a refreshing way without being judged or criticized. Here is a ritual that can help you break the mold and see yourself as a creative person. —L.N.

What You Need

- The necessary tools of your craft
- The same time set aside each week as your creative time, at least two to three hours
- A room where you can be alone or a place to make your art

What You Do

Make sure you have the tools of the trade. You can go on a shopping spree before your first creative date with yourself and buy art supplies, paper or a journal, a camera, clay, or whatever you need. Make sure you have enough material to last for a while, so you don't use the lack of supplies as an excuse to not create.

Finish ahead of time any work you need to do for your job or family, so your creative time is kept sacred. Notify family and friends that a certain time of day or night is your time. People are not to ask you out to dinner or to the movies and are not even to call during that time unless it is an emergency.

When you begin, suspend all judgment and criticism. Perhaps you will eventually be a famous artist, paid handsomely for your work, but what matters now is that you are creating something you love. You may choose to share your work with loving friends, but keep in mind that early criticism can be paralyzing. After a few months of doing your work, you may be surprised at how much better you feel about yourself and the world. This is only the beginning. Who knows where it will lead?

Seeing the Blessings

If the only prayer you say in your whole life is "thank you," that would suffice.

—Meister Eckhart

Do you ever find yourself screaming at the television or punching the newspaper? Do you rail at the world as a daily practice? I did. I was growing cynical and sad watching humankind's latest expression of inhumanity. I wasn't often thankful anymore and I didn't see much that was good.

Then, I realized that nothing that I heard or read was from my direct experience. It was all secondhand, filtered through the eyes of someone else. Without the balance of my own eyes, my own experience, I dwelt on secondhand accounts of murders, rapes, fires, and every other kind of human atrocity. Was nothing good going on?

When you expose yourself to too much bad, you eventually stop seeing any good. You start to think of the world as the thousands of ways we hurt one another. The theologian Matthew Fox suggests, "We must go blessing hunting because our culture is so steeped in cynicism and despair . . . that we have lost our awareness and even curiosity about what is good." —V.L.

What You Need

- Time in a quiet place

What You Do

Give yourself a one-week break from the news. In this week, take the time you would have spent reading the paper or watching television to take a walk and be with a friend in nature. Make a point to go blessing hunting. For a start, simply sit and reflect on these incredible thoughts from *Sins of the Spirit, Blessings of the Flesh* by Matthew Fox.

A List of Awesome Things

- In a single season, a large elm tree makes about six million leaves.

- Squashes have been measured to exert a lifting force of five thousand pounds per square inch.

- For every particle of matter there are one billion particles of light.

- Every single hydrogen atom in our bodies was once part of the Big Bang itself.
- Blood evolved directly from ancient seawater.
- In a lifetime, a heart beats about four billion times.
- With every breath, we inhale millions of molecules of sky.
- African bushmen can see four moons of Jupiter with the naked eye.
- Dogs and cats have adopted orphaned skunks or piglets.
- Year-old beavers help their parents take care of younger siblings.
- One female ocean sunfish carries three hundred million eggs.

Every day, write down just five things that were good. When a week is up, make a decision about how, when, and in what ways you wish to take in information. You may want to seek out less commercial sources of information, like National Public Radio and public television, or listen to foreign news, such as the British Broadcasting Corporation. I like to read the *New York Times'* Sunday edition. Remember to balance what you take in from outside sources with your own knowing, and to cultivate your ability to see blessings.

Waiting to Adopt

When your heart speaks, take good notes.
—Panna Flower

In the months of waiting to adopt a baby from China, I was overwhelmed with every possible emotion. It was hard enough to wait, but the not knowing was excruciating. I craved that elemental tie that birth mothers feel in their bodies, a cord that would tie me to this faraway child who was on the earth but as yet unknown to me.

One day, I received word from our translator, Xiao Ching, that a picture of our child had arrived. My husband Dean and I leaped into the car to go get it. What we got was a postage stamp–size picture, just the face of a small infant in a red quilted jacket, and the news that she was from Hunan province. Though it wasn't much, it made her real. I started to write to her and began a "conversation" that gave me great comfort in the days of waiting to go to China. When we finally met, I felt as if I had always known her.

Louise told me that my dreams and fears during this time were much like her own when she was waiting for Sarah and Laura to be born. I was becoming a mother every day of the wait, bonding to my child in my heart. —V.L.

What You Need

- Time alone, or with your spouse or partner
- A place to write, draw, or just sit in silence

What You Do

During the long days of waiting, take time to simply sit in silence for a few minutes each day, letting your heart slowly embrace your child. Contemplate the thought that you are already parents; your child is simply away from home.

If you have a picture of the child you are to adopt, make an enlarged color copy of it and put it in a prominent place. Write short messages to her and attach them to the picture. If you like to write, try crafting a poem or a love letter. If you are more visual, draw or sculpt something for her that expresses the essence of her as you see it in the picture. It will be a precious keepsake later.

Here is a poem I wrote for YuWen that really helped me make a connection to her.

Waiting for My Daughter

For YuWen

My heart sings out with longing for you,
good luck girl of the Hunan winter.
White moonbeam fingers stroke your sleeping head,
sculpt your pink ears, trace your butter brown lips.
My heart knows you China girl of black night
in the red Changsha coals that warm your small feet.
It throws a rope wide across the brave clouds,
loops your dragon soul in soft cords of love.
My heart can see you Mao's girl of no name.
It names you with salt tears that fall from my eyes.
Its long gaze embraces your strong blue-veined skull,
enfolds your soft body in long arms of hope.
My heart sings to you, puts you to sleep—
to the thunder of hummingbirds batting their wings:
their columbine nectar perfumes your sweet bed,
their gray velvet heads guard your slow, sleeping breath.
My heart awaits you, girl of ripe dreams:
the fruit will soon fall, the skin will peel open.
Come take your place in the womb of my heart:
in the mile-deep hollow of my waiting heart.

Loving Hands for a Mother-to-Be

With a child just an eye
drop away
I am the egg being timed,
the round belly of the moon
the biggest house of all.
                                    —Louise Nayer

When a woman gives birth for the first time, life changes overnight. A couple is now three and many adjustments are made to welcome a new baby into the new world. But the actual changes start much earlier in the woman's body and heart.

When I was pregnant, I was more protective of myself, just as in a number of months I would be protective of the new life outside me. My husband and I discussed finances and room changes and purchased basics for the baby-to-be. There was also fear: Would everything go all right? Would the labor be long and hard? Would the baby be healthy? Would this world be too harsh for our innocent newcomer?

Many women have strange dreams during pregnancy. I dreamt that my baby was a small black line that ran away from me in the grass. I couldn't find her and woke up sweating. Women are often afraid but don't discuss their fears. To go along with good prenatal care and regular checkups, here is a ritual that can help a pregnant woman relax and feel taken care of during one of the most vulnerable times in her life. So much of a pregnancy is spent thinking about the baby; it is good to have at least one hour a week just for the mother. —L.N.

What You Need

- A small gift such as flowers or a bar of jasmine soap
- A glass of water with a twist of lemon
- Some scented oil (lavender is nice)
- A journal

What You Do

Set aside one hour once a week for gentle massage of the expectant mother's head, shoulders, hands, legs, and feet. Make sure to make an appointment and keep it! Treat the woman like royalty as she lies down in her favorite spot, wearing loose-fitting clothes. Offer your gift.

After offering the lemon water and finding a comfortable position for her, start by gently massaging her feet with the oil. As you massage, let her know she is free to talk or simply to feel the loving hands helping her relax. Maybe she wants to cry, laugh, yawn, or simply lie still. She might not talk much during the first two or three sessions, but later she might find that this is a good time to let out feelings about the upcoming birth. Listen to her and let her know that she is safe.

End the session with a hug and a promise to massage her next week. If she wants, she can write in her journal for a short time after the massage and keep it as a diary of her feelings during this spectacular time in her life.

A Mother's First Week after Giving Birth

Let me rest and drink in this moment,
as you lie beside me, this sweet separation.
—*Virginia Lang*

My friend Rae Ling Chang is a thoroughly modern woman. Raised in Taiwan and educated in this country, she nonetheless chose to observe Chinese tradition when she had her babies. She was expected to stay in her home for a full month. She was not to shower, walk down steps, or expose herself to cold wind. Her mother fed her restorative soups and cared for the newborn while she regained her strength.

Most of my American friends delivered their babies in sterile hospital operating rooms or birthing rooms. They were discharged the same or the next day and were back to work in a matter of weeks. No one had her mother present.

Giving birth is one of the high points in a woman's life, a fragile, tender time unlike any other. Why do we rush through it as if it were only a medical event? Where is the celebration and regard for the woman who has just brought a new life into the world? —V.L.

What You Need

- A list of your favorite foods, scents, poems, and music

What You Do

During your pregnancy, develop a picture of yourself in the days after giving birth. Where are you sitting? What are you eating? What objects of beauty are in the room? Who is there? Make a list of special items you would really enjoy.

Next, ask a special person—your mother, best friend, or sister—to be your mother's helper and to stay with you as much as possible the week the baby comes home. In this culture, we are hesitant to ask for help, so ask this directly as a special request and spell out the ways you would like help. A month or so before the baby is due, take your helper on a special trip to buy some things that will make these first weeks home comfortable for you. Consider items like:

- A special down pillow
- Favorite soups to have on hand
- Scented soaps and a loofah for the bath
- Very soft slippers and feminine pajamas
- A book of poetry by Mary Oliver
- CD by Josh Groban or Andrea Bocelli

Celebrate yourself in whatever ways your taste and circumstances allow.

Waiting for a Sister or Brother

When I am singing to you
on earth all evil ends
—Gabriela Mistral

I had little understanding of the experience of being a big brother/ big sister until my daughter, Sarah, became an older sibling. We read her a book, *I Want to Tell You about My Baby*, that helped tremendously. We also talked to her often during the pregnancy to ease the transition. She even talked to my tummy and began her own relationship with her sister-to-be. Though my children fight at times, I am happy that their relationship has been unusually close.

My sister told me about a boy who sang to his pregnant mom for many months. The baby in the womb loved the song "You Are My Sunshine." The mom said the baby moved back and forth in her tummy when the little boy sang.

Sadly, after the baby girl was born, she was very ill. The nurses told the parents she might die. The little boy kept insisting he wanted to sing to his baby, but no one would let him into the hospital nursery. Out of desperation and wanting to please their son, the parents finally got clearance, and the little boy, only three years old, sang to his dying sister.

He sang many times, and her body began to stir. A few days later, she began to recover. Was it his singing? Perhaps. —L.N.

What You Need

- A special song picked by the firstborn child

What You Do

After you tell the older child of the pregnancy, have him sing a special song to the baby as often as possible. This can also be snuggle time for him. The song can be made up or one that the child knows from school or home.

After the baby is born, print out the words to the song on a sheet of colored paper. Have the child decorate it. Take a picture of the child and baby and frame the song and picture. Hang the song and picture over the older child's bed.

Special Time for an Older Child

For Sarah

You are the universe: the sun, the sky, the moon. Let me see your hands, like no other's, the way the lines are deep, the way they curve, like no other's.

—Louise Nayer

When my daughter Laura was born, we gave my older daughter, Sarah, a table and chairs and signed the gift from Laura. Sarah was thrilled—and even more thrilled when friends came and took her to the zoo and out for ice cream. Often when a baby is born, the older child or children need to feel included and that they are still precious beings. It is important that close friends and family remember the older child by bringing small gifts. Sometimes, these gifts can be brought to the baby shower; at other times, handed to the older child on a separate occasion.

Think about your older child, what she likes to do, her favorite places to visit, her favorite foods. She will be thrilled to go out for a milkshake with mom, dad, or a trusted adult once a week. Keep the attention focused on your child—no phones or reading the paper. Even if the child says nothing but simply enjoys scooping the whipped cream off the milkshake and knowing you are there, that is enough. —L.N.

What You Need

- Special time set aside
- A calendar picked out by your older child

What You Do

Near the time of the delivery, family and close friends can take the older child aside and make some dates on a calendar. Everyone can find one to two hours during the first month after the baby is born. Perhaps they can take a trip to the zoo or walk down the street for an ice-cream cone. It doesn't have to take a lot of time or money, but these special moments can be an opportunity for the older child to have time away from the busy household and to get some extra attention.

Parents can also make dates; the mom can do this when she feels stronger, so the child can look forward to special time with mom and dad as well. Some families continue the ritual with each child every week or two. It helps each child feel loved and reduces sibling rivalry!

New Parents Learning from the Past

The lines on your hand stop and start like pilgrimages.
—Louise Nayer

My father loves language and poetry. I remember him reading Shakespeare to me when I was young and endlessly reciting Keats: "The beaded bubbles winking at the brim." This inspired my own writing.

My mother was always organized and forever practical. I rebelled against her practicality for many years, but I now fully appreciate what she taught me.

One way to think about how to parent our own children is to reflect on how our parents and other adults enriched us and helped us evolve into full human beings. Here is a ritual to help expectant mothers and fathers make conscious choices about what they want to pass on to the next generation. —L.N.

What You Need

- A dinner-table conversation once a week before a baby is born or before a child enters a home through adoption
- Photos of memorable times in your childhood with a parent or favorite adult
- An agreement to focus on parenting

What You Do

Think about specific people from your childhood and what they did that helped you grow and made you happy. Perhaps your mom ordered all your favorite food at a restaurant and then told you how beautiful you looked, or your dad read poetry to you before bed.

Specific aunts, uncles, or family friends may have played roles in your life: taught you about art, showed you how to jump the waves beyond the breakers, or simply sat with you and let you talk about your day. What do these moments have in common? How can you recreate these kinds of moments for your own child?

During one or more of the conversations, contemplate a photograph of an adult who was special to you. What qualities did that person possess? What can you learn from her life? Perhaps one person taught you courage, while another gave you many compliments and made you feel good about yourself. Perhaps a teacher opened you up to the vast world of art and literature, or a grandfather listened to you when it seemed everyone else was too busy.

If you wish, write down the names of specific people and the qualities that were important to you. You can create a collage of photos and words and reflect on it as you become a mom or a dad.

Beginning Life in a New Home

Home is the place where when you go there,
they have to take you in.
                                        —Robert Frost

When we bought our home in Wallingford, Pennsylvania, we learned that only two families had owned it in eighty-five years: John and Sarah Albert's family and Dr. Donald and Nancy Patterson's family. When we moved in, I felt the presence of these families and so many other people in this home we were now to occupy. Children were born here, cats and dogs were raised here, friends were welcomed here, elders died here. The place vibrated with memories, both good and bad.

We spent so long working out the details of the sale—the finances, the title insurance, the mortgage, the escrow terms—that we gave little time to the actual feelings associated with handing over the home from the Patterson family to ours. I began to feel better after writing to Dr. Patterson (his wife, Nancy, had died) and telling him how excited we were about the house he had loved and lived in happily for thirty years. He wrote back to tell me how pleased he was that I loved it, too.

The night after we moved in, I sat in front of the first fire we lit in the hearth and "talked" to Sarah Albert and Nancy Patterson. I told them I would be taking care of the house now but would always honor their memories here. As I finished speaking, a large log split open and fell with a huge burst of light emanating from its middle.

Wherever you choose to live, someone has been there before, someone who called the place home. Here is a ritual to honor the space of others and all the memories that fill a space. —V.L.

What You Need

- The first night in a new home or apartment
- A fireplace or a scented candle

What You Do

Light a fire or the candle and sit quietly, thinking about the people who lived in the home before you. If you have a photograph of them, hold it in your hand.

Say silently or aloud, "I accept responsibility for the care of this home and will honor the memories of all those who have lived here before me. May this home be a place of happiness and peace."

If you are the first to occupy a new home, you might say, "I am grateful for the many hands that built this home, and I now accept responsibility for its care. May this home be a place of happiness and peace."

Beginning to Serve Yourself

Alone now, I can hear bells from a far-off village where an old woman bathes me in light. "Eat well," she says, stroking my long hair, giving me a rose and handing me warm bread and honey.

—Louise Nayer

Most of us have loved and lost and at some time in our lives felt overwhelming grief and loneliness. We think, "Will I ever get over these feelings? Will I be alone now forever?" Friends tell us of support groups at churches and synagogues, and of new classes at college. They encourage us with well-meaning suggestions "to get out and smell the roses" and that "there are more fish in the sea."

Though it is important to get out and live life again, it is equally important to experience our grief and to slow down, take a deep breath, and take care of ourselves, whatever life holds for us. For many of us who have been serving others, it is crucial that we learn how to care for ourselves.

What You Need

- Soothing music
- Your favorite food for a meal (you may want to pick out a new recipe that looks especially appealing)
- A decorative place mat and linen napkin
- Utensils
- A wine glass (for any drink you choose)
- A candle

What You Do

While the soothing music plays, prepare a meal for yourself with patience and love. Thoughts of sadness or "Why am I cooking if it's for just myself?" might surface, but push them away with thoughts of "I'm taking good care of myself." Set the table with the place mat, linen napkin, utensils, and wine glass. When the meal is ready, take it to the table and pour your drink. Light the candle and take a deep breath, saying, "I'm happy to be taking care of myself so well. I deserve the best!"

Fabulous Firsts

First steps, first school, first job, first kiss: We can never again capture the excitement, the range of emotion, the sheer drama of the firsts in our lives. And yet it is so easy to overlook these poignant moments, to let them go unmarked, uncelebrated.

With just a little thought, we can frame these moments in ceremony, preserving their uniqueness in our memories like wild violets pressed in an old dog-eared book.

First Day of School for a Preschooler

When the first baby laughed for the first time, the laugh broke into a thousand pieces and they all went skipping about, and that was the beginning of fairies.

—J. M. Barrie

What is more precious than the laughter of a child, the total abandon and head-flinging joy of pure glee? The first few years in the life of a child are so magical and so special that it can be heart-wrenching to leave this time behind for the more practical, socialized world of school.

On YuWen's first day of preschool, Dean and I went with her, holding her hand and trying desperately not to look at each other as our eyes welled up with tears. As much as we liked Montessori Children's House, we knew this entry into the "real" world would slowly move her from her magical life to one of limits, rules, and realities. We just weren't ready. Is anyone? —V.L.

What You Need

- Time to transition
- A soft felt heart cut into two pieces or a napkin

What You Do

First, be certain to give yourself enough time to spend ten to twenty minutes of transition time at your child's school. For many days after YuWen started school, she would say, "Will you get me started?" After a short game or puzzle, she would be ready to join in with others.

Once you see that your child is able to make this transition, tell her to look in her pocket for a small piece of felt that is soft and has a message from you on it. "I am with you in my heart" is a good one. Show her that you have the other half of the heart in your pocket, and tell her that you will always return to complete the heart every day. When you pick her up, match the hearts together and let her see that you have been missing her just as much as she has been missing you.

You may also want to draw a simple heart on her lunch napkin that day—or any day—as a reminder that your hearts are always joined.

First Day Back to School

Inchworm, inchworm
Measuring the marigolds
—Frank Loesser

A colleague of mine at City College of San Francisco told me about this simple ritual that she does each year with her children. At the beginning of the summer, she plants her garden. At the end of the summer, when the garden is in full bloom, she snaps a photo of each child by a favorite apple tree on the first day of school. The family can measure how the children have grown by how tall they are next to the tree. Just as the garden grows throughout the summer, the children are part of nature, growing and blossoming in their own ways. This is a way of commemorating the first day of school. —L.N.

What You Need

- An outdoor site for snapping photos
- A camera

- Something from the garden
- A photo album

What You Do

Each year on the first day of school, take your children into the backyard for a photo shoot. Ask them to stand next to a favorite tree or bush, something that will allow you to see how tall they have grown since the previous year. Take their picture, and give them something from the garden, such as a leaf or a small pod, to take with them to school. Add the picture to a photo album containing the pictures from past years.

Young Child's First Performance

Bright light, star of night, dance with joy.
—Louise Nayer

Fear of public speaking has been said to be matched only by fear of death. For children, recitals, dance concerts, plays, and the like can carry a similar weight.

We all have stories of the results of this fear. A boy named Johnny in my fourth-grade class urinated onstage to his horror and to the horror of sixty pairs of eyes staring at him. There are many other tales of upset stomachs, tears, even fainting. Sometimes, young girls in butterfly costumes dash to mommy or daddy when the lights dim.

How do we encourage our children to let their lights shine, have fun, and leave room for mistakes? If a five-year-old does run to mom and dad and misses the performance, is that so terrible?

Also, how do we honor all the children who perform while giving our own young person some special attention? —L.N.

What You Need

- Extra time with your child the night before
- Examples of people who performed and sometimes made mistakes, either from your own life or the lives of friends
- A bouquet of flowers for every child (donated by all the parents)

What You Do

First, make a commitment to attend the performance and include special others whom your child suggests. If your child is in grade school, don't dwell on or talk too much about the upcoming performance except to work out all the details.

The night before the big day, spend some extra time with your child. Relate a story about how you performed in a recital that may not have gone perfectly. Keep it light: "I forgot my comb, so my hair stood up on end" or "I missed a few lines and the stage was very quiet for a while, but we managed to finish the show."

Make it clear that you respect all the hard work your child has done to prepare for this performance. Try to connect with other parents through the teacher, and as a group contribute money for a small bouquet for each child, to be presented at the end of the performance.

Go out for pizza or ice cream with family and friends and offer a toast to your child for all the hard work, however the performance went.

First Time at Sleep-Away Camp

Mommy, I love you with two hearts.
—YuWen

When I was nine, my city school had a one-week program for fourth graders to get us out in the country. I got strep throat two days before the bus left and was driven up later by my mother. I vividly remember the moment she left me and drove back to Manhattan.

When I was ten, I went to a church camp for one month. During the first week, I was so anxious that I stayed up until midnight, sitting in a big armchair in the common room. When the camp director made his rounds, he was surprised to see me completely awake.

Not every child has trouble with leaving home, but homesickness at camp is so common that most camps don't allow phone calls except in emergencies because they fear that children will fall apart when they hear their parents' voices. Many children are anxious, but most get over it and have a wonderful time making friends, playing in the great outdoors, and gradually learning to separate from their parents.

How do we make the transition to camp easier for a first-timer? Even if the child has friends or siblings going with him, getting on the bus to go far away can be a frightening experience. —L.N.

What You Need

- Photos of the family, including the family pets
- Flat stones
- A red marker

What You Do

At dinnertime a couple of days before the trip, bring out some photos of the family and the family pets that you will give to your child for the trip. You can put them in a small photo album that your child can look at on the bus ride and keep nearby in his cabin.

Go together to find special stones to represent you and your child to be used as "touchstones." Draw hearts on each stone with the marker. Give the stone you selected to represent yourself to your child and vice versa. One or both parents can do this.

Tell your child that while he is away he should hold your touchstone in his hand every night before he goes to sleep and remember that you are holding his stone and saying goodnight to him. "When you hold the stone, think of me and know that every day I send my love to you as I hold my stone and kiss you goodnight."

Teen's First Job

Let me grow. Hold on. Let me be free.
And please always see the good in me.
—Louise Nayer

Most of us worked as teens, whether it was babysitting, mowing lawns, or serving ice cream at the local Dairy Queen. Perhaps the job didn't pay very much, but the act of getting to work on time, doing what was asked, and bringing home a paycheck is an important transition in a teen's life and should be recognized.

Teenagers often get a bad rap, but there are many dedicated and responsible young people in the world. My daughters and friends of theirs clean up beaches, go on AIDS marches, and sometimes donate their allowances to good causes. They also get to work on time and do a good job. How can we honor our teens when most of them don't want to be fussed over, especially by mom and dad? Here is a simple ritual that can earn them some extra money, a bit of an education, and respect. —L.N.

What You Need

- Your teen's favorite meal and sparkling cider
- A paycheck
- A Roth IRA application

What You Do

At the end of the first pay period, cook your teen's favorite meal and offer a sparkling cider toast to a job well done. After dinner, present your child with an application form for a Roth IRA and agree to match her first paycheck with an equal amount of cash.

Show her the math: If she puts just $100 in the IRA at age sixteen, assuming 11 percent compounded interest, she will have $16,627 by age sixty-five. If she makes $2,000 over the summer and puts her full summer's earnings into the IRA, she will have $332,549, tax-free, by age sixty-five. If she likes math, she may want to do other projections. Explain to her that while money should not rule her life, it can make her life comfortable and allow her to help others as well.

Be a good role model for your teen. Show her how you save money each month, even if it's just the change in your wallet. Show her also how you use some of your money to help others.

First-Time Driver

Hold fast to the steering.
Stay awake,
even with all the shadows
of night.
We, who love you,
fill the air
with soft whispers:
love, be safe.

—Louise Nayer

Children are the future, the hope of the world, the most precious beings to their parents. In this country, at sixteen years old, young people get into powerful metal machines and begin adult lives on the road. It can be a terrifying road, with speeders, drunk drivers, and road rage. When I faced my own fifteen-year-old who got a permit in San Francisco, I was aware of the need to trust her for the responsible person she was and wanted to create a ritual within our family to remind us of the importance of this milestone and that our hearts are always with our newest driver. —L.N.

What You Need

- Your teen's favorite dinner
- The successfully passed written driver's test from the Department of Motor Vehicles
- A contract between parents and teen
- A copy of the Prayer for the Road

What You Do

Make your child's favorite dinner the day she receives her driver's license. Ask her ahead of time to bring home the written driver's test as a memento.

Write a contract with her, spelling out specific expectations of her use of the car. Make two copies of the contract and read it out loud to her at the end of the meal, with parents and child signing it and placing it somewhere safe.

Sample Contract

Respecting the privilege of driving, I will:

- Wear a seatbelt and ask my passengers to do the same.
- Drive at or under the posted speed limit.
- Respect the rules of the road.
- Drive with courtesy and caution.
- Be home on time or call before I am late.
- Take care of the car, reporting problems immediately.
- Refuse to drink or use any drugs when driving.

We will:

- Expect to be called if any problem with the car or passengers arises.
- Come get you, no questions asked, when you need us.
- Always take care of repairs needed on the car.

Together, read out loud the Prayer for the Road or a special prayer you make up as a family. Place the prayer near where she picks up the car keys, and place one copy of the prayer in the glove compartment.

End the evening by telling your child how proud you are that she has successfully reached this milestone in her life.

Prayer for the Road

May you, your car, and all your passengers, day and night,
    be safe, sober, and alert
looking out for any who may endanger you.
May you never rush
for your life is more precious
than any missed appointment.
May you always care for your car
for it takes precious cargo.
May you always use good thinking
and know that you are always
in our hearts as you go
on your journeys
from place to place.
May you always arrive
safely at your destination.

First-Generation College Graduate

*As we let our light shine, we unconsciously give other
people permission to do the same.*

—*Nelson Mandela*

I grew up with college-educated parents who expected that I would
graduate from college, but the students I teach come from families where they are usually the first to finish college. They are the
trailblazers.

Graduating from college is a big step for anyone, especially
those who are first-generation grads. Most of my students at City
College in San Francisco work thirty hours a week and take a full
load of classes. Some also have family responsibilities. Pursuing

a degree is a difficult road with few markers and sometimes not enough support. Too often, there is the temptation to quit school.

Many graduates are too busy with work and school to take much time out to acknowledge this significant step in their families' histories. They may even feel disconnected from their families as they begin new lives.

Often, relatives cannot attend graduation ceremonies because they live far away or the school issues limited invitations, so it is important to plan a special celebration to let the graduate know how this achievement honors the whole family. —L.N.

What You Need

- A gathering of supportive family and friends
- The name of a special teacher who helped along the way

What You Do

One friend or relative should host a special dinner for the graduate and invite family members and friends who have helped the student along the way. Ask the graduate to name teachers who were especially important, perhaps an elementary school teacher or a college professor.

If possible, invite the teachers to the gathering. Any teacher would be thrilled at the invitation. If a teacher lives far away, the graduate can write a letter with the good news. If the teacher is deceased, ask the graduate to speak about the teacher and why she should be remembered. Prepare a toast to the graduate, given by family members and friends expressing their pride in her accomplishments.

At the party, encourage the graduate to pick a person in the family to mentor, perhaps a young person who is having difficulties in school. A first-generation college graduate may inspire other family members to pursue their dreams, even late in life.

First-Time Voter

Lift every voice and sing.
—James Weldon Johnson

My grandmother was a suffragette in upstate New York. My mother also worked for the rights of women as a nurse and as the editor of a nursing journal. They both passed down to me a legacy of social action and the need to be informed and to have a voice through voting.

For years, my husband registered voters; I helped him, going door-to-door in San Francisco neighborhoods, encouraging people to go to the polls. There are many important measures to vote for, some in fine print—like keeping libraries open for longer hours, funding neighborhood community centers, or creating small class sizes in schools. The bills that get passed have profound effects on the lives of ordinary people. Here is a practice to help a new voter begin a lifelong ritual of participation in the community. —L.N.

What You Need

- A voter registration packet
- A file folder marked "voting"
- The local newspaper for the day of your first vote

What You Do

A month before your first-time trip to the polls, go over your voter registration packet with family and friends. Discuss the issues, remembering that people have the freedom to express differing views on all issues.

Study the issues over dinner at a local restaurant. Make this an annual gathering. Perhaps one of your parents or an uncle or aunt can go over your packet with you.

If you live in an area with district elections of representatives, call their offices directly and say, "I am a first-time voter. What are you doing for our district?" You may be surprised at the quick response.

After voting, set up a file with your first registration booklet and any letters you received from senators or representatives. You can also write down any referendum bills that you voted for that passed and had a positive effect on your life. Pass this file down to your children, nieces, nephews, or to a young person in your life who is going to the polls for the first time. Also, save the newspaper of the first day that you went to the polls. Your voting folder is a keepsake and a reminder to others that you took your vote seriously.

You are now a voting citizen and can make a pledge to yourself to continue to be informed, to vote, and to get others to do the same.

First Apartment

I get by with a little help from my friends.
—Ringo Starr

When two people marry, all sorts of things happen to support their newly independent life together. There are showers, beautiful gifts, dinners, and shopping sprees. But when a person begins an independent life, usually nothing happens at all! Why is that? Many young men and women do not have partners or do not have traditional marriages. Too often, wonderful people are unwittingly punished in our culture for their lifestyle choices.

This ritual is a way to celebrate an important milestone in the life of a friend or partners who are not getting married in a traditional wedding. This will help them feel loved and supported.

What You Need

- A pen and paper
- Gifts for the apartment, both practical and beautiful
- Framed photos of close friends
- The verse "Friendship" by George Eliot in calligraphy, attractively framed

What You Do

Make a list of useful items needed to set up housekeeping for the first time. These will include nonstick pots and pans, flatware, glassware, a toaster, a blender, everyday china, a shower curtain, flower pots—many of the same things couples need. Be sure to include items that are not only practical, but beautiful.

At a meeting arranged by a close friend, assign one well-organized person the task of coordinating a moving-in shower to be held just before or just after the guest of honor moves. The organizer should call to ask each shower guest to "register" for an item on the master list. Each person should also bring a framed photo of himself to the celebratory shower.

At the shower, ask each guest to present his gift and photo with a personal toast acknowledging this new step in his friend's life and offering his love and support. As each person finishes speaking, ask him to place his photo on a designated table, mantle, or wall. The framed copy of George Eliot's statement on friendship may be placed in the center, with the friends' photos around it as a "circle of friends."

> Friendship is the comfort, the inexpressible comfort
> of feeling safe with a person
> having neither to weigh thoughts nor measure words
> but pouring all right out as they are,
> chaff and grain together, certain that a faithful

friendly hand will take and sift them, keep
what is worth keeping, and with a breath of comfort,
blow the rest away.

—George Eliot

Red-Letter Days

Certain days are cause for great celebration: going off to college, finding a job, finding a partner, having a child, retiring. These are moments to cherish, and the attention we give to them has lasting effects on our lives, helping us tuck away loving memories, reserves we can draw on during difficult times.

We honor ourselves and those around us when we take the time to mark these events, engraving on our hearts and minds the importance of what has happened on these days.

An Adoption Ceremony

My heart knows you China girl of black night
in the red Changsha coals that warm your small feet.
It throws a rope wide across the brave clouds,
loops your dragon soul in soft cords of love.

—Virginia Lang

When we brought YuWen home from China, we held a break-of-day ceremony on a rocky cliff overlooking the Pacific Ocean. She was dressed in a red Chinese silk gown adorned with little gold bears and was surrounded by people close to our family.

Louise and "Godfather Jim" read beautiful pieces they had written, and our friend Claude read "The Song of Pure Happiness," a very old Chinese poem by Li Po. Another friend, Judy Kimmel, rang a Tibetan bell, and one of my godchildren, Morgan Green, handed out red flowers for each person to present to YuWen.

Then, we all walked together down to the ocean and let the soft curling waves of the Pacific tickle her tiny feet. As we looked out over the ocean to her first home so far away, I was struck by how very different her life would be on this side of the ocean. I was very moved by this heartfelt dedication by the people who would now come to know and care for her as family.

Afterward, we shared a festive brunch given by our friends the Greens, and everyone got a chance to hold and play with YuWen, who was ten months old at the time. —V.L.

What You Need

- A special fabric or color from the child's birth country
- A setting in nature
- A small gathering of family and friends

- Selected readings, music, and flowers that reflect her heritage

What You Do

If you sew or know someone who can, make a special dedication outfit in the spirit of the child's native country. In China, red is the color of celebration. The flag of California, her new home, inspired the little golden bears on YuWen's gown.

Choose a setting in nature that has meaning for you. Ask close friends and family to attend a ceremony there and bring something that is special to them—perhaps a bell, a flower, or a poem. Let each person read, sing, or play an instrument according to her abilities. The youngest in the group may want to offer to each person a flower native to the child's country of birth.

Join hands and say together, "Respecting the life and lineage of this child, we receive her gladly into this culture, this family, and these hearts. May the richness of her native culture be the seed that bears fruit in the fertile soil of our lives." Observe a minute of silence together. Then, celebrate with a meal that includes food from both cultures. In Chinese tradition, long noodles are eaten for long life.

Here is a poem I wrote for YuWen:

> A far wind blows
> through your round flesh,
> covers the oceans,
> warms my long bones.
> Your small heart beats
> in the gold summer light,
> in the long Yiyang shadows,
> in the blaze of noon sun.
> I need no compass
> to find your boned hand,
> no rod to divine
> your soft parting lips.

We walk in locked step,
through the caverns of time,
through the mighty black ocean,
through the blue peacock sky.

Here is a Native American adoption blessing:

Friend, this day I take you in my arms and hug you strongly.
And if it is meant to be,
Our Father the sun will, in his path over the world,
rise and reach his zenith,
Hold himself firmly and smile upon you and me
that our roads of life may be finished.
Here I touch you with my hand
and with the hands and hearts of the gods.
I pray to the wind of life,
That our roads of life may be finished together.
Friend, may the light of the gods meet you!

Here is a beautiful blessing translated from the original Bengali by
Rabindranath Tagore:

Bless this little heart, this white soul
that has won the kiss of heaven for
our earth.
He loves the light of the sun, he loves the
sight of his mother's face.
He has not learned to despise the dust, and
to hanker after gold.
Clasp him to your heart and bless him.
He has come into this land of a hundred crossroads.
I know not how he chose you from the
crowd, came to your door, and grasped your
hand to ask his way.
He will follow you, laughing and talking,

and not a doubt in his heart.
Keep his trust, lead him straight and
bless him.
Lay your hand on his head, and pray that
though the waves underneath grow threatening,
yet the breath from above may come and
fill his sails and waft him to the haven of peace.
Forget him not in your hurry, let him come
to your heart and bless him.

Choosing a Spiritual Mentor

Be ye lamps unto yourselves, be your own confidence.
Hold to the truth within yourselves as to the only lamp.
—Buddhist saying

When my daughters Sarah and Laura were eight and six, Ginny and Dean's home was a special haven to them. Ginny and Dean cooked many elegant dinners for special occasions, and at a young age, the girls were allowed to handle crystal glasses filled with sparkling apple cider.

Ginny's family also came to the children's soccer games and piano and dance recitals, and threw parties that included my parents, then in their eighties. It was certainly a merging of two families and of all the generations. It was only natural that Ginny and Dean would become Sarah and Laura's godparents.

Many families pick godparents for their children through a church christening and naming ceremony, bringing their children into their religious tradition. We attended a Unitarian Universalist church, but there was no formal godparent ritual, so we created our own. This ritual can be for families not involved with a place of worship or for godparents who were present at a church ceremony but want to rededicate themselves to their godchildren, making a commitment to now older children that they will be involved in their lives continuously. —L.N.

What You Need

- Godparents, a godchild, and the godchild's family
- Readings written or selected by both families
- A special dinner
- Formal clothes for the event
- Special gifts to give the children as keepsakes

What You Do

Choose an evening for the ceremony and prepare by writing or finding selected readings. The meal can be shared, each family cooking one or two dishes. It adds importance to the evening if everyone dresses in his finest and sets the table elegantly.

After the meal and before dessert, begin the readings. Let each person read a favorite poem or passage or say something heartfelt.

After the readings, the godparents and family stand up and read words of commitment to the godchild. The words can serve as a reminder of their deep promise to hold the child in their hearts and minds and to guide her as she grows into a fully developed human being. You may choose to use the words that we did:

"We promise to love and guide you without judgment, to listen to your deepest feelings, and to help you find your purpose in life. We will always be there as extra shoulders to lean on when times are tough. Call on us. We embrace all of you, everything you feel, everything you think, and everything you will become."

Any kind of special object can be then passed to the children: a book, a painting, a necklace, or something from nature like a stone or a shell.

After the readings, serve cake and spend the evening doing what the families like to do best. Our families sang and played piano into the evening.

Honoring Special People in the Lives of Families

With love, all turmoil ceased.
—Gabriela Mistral

There is always enough love to go around. Many of us remember special adults from our childhood who were not relatives, but who visited us and gave us special attention. Perhaps they played blocks with us upstairs, read us stories, taught us how to French braid our hair, or babysat from time to time.

In our family, "Uncle" Bill taught Sarah and Laura to be artists, spending countless hours drawing with them. He also taught them how to garden. One dear friend, Nancy, decorated sugar cookies with them each year for Christmas. With her environmental expertise, she also took us all on hikes, introducing the kids to the tide pools by Año Nuevo State Reserve in Pescadero, California.

Families can be quite insular, protective, and sometimes jealous of outside influences, but when a trusted close friend enters a family, wonderful exchanges can happen. The children receive more love, and the parents get needed breaks from the demands of family life.

We can honor these special people for all they do for the children and the whole family. We can also remind our families how important they are to the lives of special friends. This ritual is one way to honor these friends and welcome them into the family. —L.N.

What You Need

- The friend's favorite foods
- A photo album with pictures taken over time
- A handmade card

What You Do

Invite your friend over for her favorite dinner, prepared by the whole family. You can make it special by dressing up and setting the table as you might for a holiday. On the handmade card, ask everyone to write something about why the friend is important to them: "I love the paint set you bought me and love to draw with you" or "I love the walks we take at Point Reyes National Seashore and will remember the dappled horses we saw along the way." Give your friend the photo album, including photos of the family with her. Promise to keep adding to it as you create more memories. Give the card and afterward offer a toast: "You are family!"

A Father-and-Son Pilgrimage

I am on my way running, I am on my way running,
Looking toward me is the edge of the world,
I am trying to reach it,
The edge of the world does not look far away,
To that I am on my way running.

—Anonymous

When my friend Peter Borenstein was a young man, his father, Mark, took him to the gravesite of Peter's great-grandfather in Poland. Most of the family was killed in World War II, so it was a particularly moving pilgrimage for father and son.

I was struck by how deeply Mark felt about making this trip with Peter and how rich it was for Peter to see not only his place in the Borenstein family, but in the history of the world. Forging an identity is so critical in the development of children, yet many of us have no rite of passage for a child that invites him to take his place and to see that place as important. —V.L.

What You Need

* Pictures, letters, and memorabilia from the past

What You Do

Choose a day such as the anniversary of a grandparent's death to talk to your son about his family history. Take out pictures and letters and, if possible, invite elders to recount stories from the past.

During a vacation, take a trip to the birthplace of his grandparents or to the cemetery where they are buried, where you may make a rubbing of the tombstone together. Help your child to see those who came before him as real people whose characters and personalities are parts of him.

At a special shared meal, give him something that was special to his grandfather, such as a favorite book, a special woodworking tool, a baptism certificate, or a pocket watch. This gift is a symbol of trust. With it, include a letter to the son, letting him know how you feel about him and sharing your hopes for his future. Let him know he honors the family in all he does, but he is free to be himself and to reach beyond the limits of the past as well.

Going Off to College

It is a matter of transitions, you see; the changing, the becoming must be cared for closely.

—Leslie Marmon Silko

After my friend Kathy Martin put her son, Jeff, on a plane to Columbia University in New York City, she went home and cleaned his room for hours, just sobbing and sobbing. After so much anticipation during his senior year, she was exhausted and had not had time to take in the feelings of this important transition in both her life and Jeff's life.

When a child leaves home, there is such a mix of feelings— sadness that a chapter is closing, joy that the child has reached an important milestone, fear of the child's future without parents standing by, hope that what has been taught will serve to support the child in his independent life. If we have done well, our children will honor us all with their intelligent choices and strong bodies. —V.L.

What You Need

- A gathering of close friends and family
- A celebratory meal
- A camera
- Personal letters

What You Do

Invite close friends and family to a sendoff dinner at the young person's home. After dinner, gather in a circle and light a candle to be passed around. Ask each person to take the candle in hand and speak from her heart words of blessing, congratulation, loss, whatever she is feeling. Then, offer a toast such as this one: "We trust you to make good choices, to honor your body, to engage your mind, to follow your dream. Go forward in love and light, knowing we hold you in our hearts with every step you take."

Take pictures of each person at the dinner. Later, frame the photos or cut and paste them into a collage. You may want to add personal sentiments under each picture or a group wish such as "We love you and trust you. We are with you in spirit every day of your life." This will remind the new student of all the love and support that go with him to his new dormitory room.

If photos are a challenge, ask each person to bring to the gathering a personal letter to the student to be put in a scrapbook for reading during the often lonely first year away from home.

Finding Your Strength in an Interview

For Laura

She carries all creatures in her soul.
She is a hawk, a fly, a cat, a minotaur.
                                        —Louise Nayer

After having had a series of rats, parakeets, and goldfish because I didn't think my allergies could withstand a furry beast, we got our dog a year ago. I've been amazed, as has my husband, at how much our dog adds to all of our lives, allowing us to shower our affection on a fuzzy being, who responds in kind.

Penny, our bichon frisé, also gives us strength. When the children feel sad, they hug her to them and she licks their faces. When we are happy, we throw her ball down our long hallway and watch her endless puppy energy.

Animals can help people's lives in all sorts of ways—even imaginary animals! When I interviewed for my position at City College of San Francisco, my friend Jeri suggested I imagine a lion going with me. —L.N.

What You Need

- A scheduled interview
- A good imagination

What You Do

As much as a week before your interview, imagine that you have a lion by your side, giving you strength and courage. Close your eyes and see its full hair and long mane.

On the day of the interview, be sure to keep your lion with you, even if you are called into the "hot room" quickly or the room is crowded and the lion has no room to lie down. I placed him by my feet, under the table, with his head up, alert and completely ready to give me the strength I needed. Other friends who have gone for interviews have also conjured up an image of the lion and presented themselves with great strength to their prospective employers.

The Wedding Tree

Our roots are with each other, now,
in the veins of the tree, in the glistening earth.
—Louise Nayer

When my stepdaughter, Bonnie, and George got married, they followed an old Quaker tradition and planted a tree in their backyard to symbolize their marriage and how it would grow over time.

The wedding was a flurry of activity, with people flying in from all over the country, many relatives from both sides, friends, and a party at their house the night before the ceremony. One of the most tranquil moments for Bonnie and George was planting the tree in the backyard, while a few people watched.

Bonnie says that, to this day, whatever else is going on in her life, she always remembers to water the tree and often looks at it, watching it grow, knowing that it symbolizes her marriage to George. Family and friends who know of the tree also have a special feeling for it, even those who live far away from Bonnie and George's backyard, as we do. —L.N.

What You Need

- A tree to plant that is appropriate for weather conditions in your area
- A shovel

What You Do

If you are leaving for your honeymoon immediately after the wedding or commitment ceremony, choose a time before the big day when you can both be present to plant the tree. You can dig together or ask for help. Gather a few special people around to watch the tree planting.

When the tree is placed in the ground, you may choose to say a few words such as these: "We promise to water and care for this tree every day and in all types of weather, as we will care for each other."

Let there be a few minutes of silence in the Quaker tradition. If you live in an apartment, you may purchase an indoor tree, such as a bonsai. You may also find a public or private place that allows tree planting and perform your ceremony there.

Celebrating Your Anniversary

Hereafter, in a better world than this,
I shall desire more love and knowledge of you.
—William Shakespeare

I've always thought an anniversary should amount to more than a dinner out. As each year of married life passes, one should get the opportunity to renew the contract or at least renegotiate the terms. No job description stays the same, so why should the job description for a spouse or partner remain fixed? It takes great communication and self-respect to keep a love relationship alive over the years. Sometimes we forget that both individuals must thrive. —V.L.

What You Need

- Two evenings before your anniversary
- The willingness to be direct

What You Do

Two nights before your anniversary, write letters to each other focusing only on the good things that have happened to you in the past year of marriage. Exchange letters and allow yourself to feel whatever is there; if it was a difficult year, you may simply want to express gratitude for the support of your partner during this time. Celebrate this in some fashion, with a dinner out or a good bottle of wine.

The next night, write letters asking for help to improve something about your life together. Do you need more help with the children? Would you like to spend more time with friends? Is money a constant worry? Exchange letters again and discuss your feelings. There may not be easy solutions, but bringing your deepest feelings to light is essential if you are to strengthen your commitment to each other. Write in the first person, such as: "I would like more time to paint."

On the anniversary itself, exchange gifts (no toasters, please). Give careful thought to what would mean the most to the other person, and forgo items you need for the house. Consider "adventure gifts" you may never have purchased before, like a hike at sunrise with a thermos of coffee, a Swedish massage for two, a poetry reading in which you offer one perfect rose, a handwritten poem, or a promise of a date night once a week.

Make your gift as personal and intimate as possible. One of the most beautiful poems I know, a romantic seventeenth-century piece, is an excellent gift for a woman who enjoys a long and mature marriage to give to her husband. I include it here for any woman lucky enough to feel this way.

To My Dear and Loving Husband

If ever two were one, then surely we.
If ever man were lov'd by wife, then thee;
If ever wife was happy in a man,
Compare with me ye women if you can.
I prize thy love more than whole Mines of gold,
Or all the riches that the East doth hold.
My love is such that Rivers cannot quench,
Nor ought but love from thee, give recompence.
Thy love is such I can no way repay,
The heavens reward thee manifold I pray.
Then while we live, in love let's so persevere,
That when we live no more, we may live ever.

—Anne Bradstreet

Here is a short but moving poem for a lover to offer.

Old Song

Take off your clothes, love,
And come to me.
Soon will the sun be breaking
Over yon sea.
And all of our hairs be white, love,
For aught we do.
And all of our nights be one, love,
For all we knew.

—Robert Creeley

A Birthday Tribute

No spring, nor summer beauty hath such grace,
As I have seen in one autumnal face.

—*John Donne*

It is sad to admit that our culture associates aging with loss. After a certain age, birthdays are often greeted with crude jokes about crow's feet, hair loss, and other declining capacities. We focus more on what we cannot do than what we have become.

When we see the beautiful autumnal face of a woman whose life has been richly lived, we know there is much to celebrate and acknowledge on the day of her birth. Here is a ritual intended to honor an older woman for all she brings to the lives of those who love her. It works for men, too.

What You Need

- A blank journal
- A person to act as coordinator
- A pen

What You Do

If the elder is fortunate to live near most of her friends and family, buy a blank journal and paste a recent photo of the honoree on its cover. With the help of an organized family coordinator, circulate the journal among the honoree's dear friends and family members.

Ask each person to write about a quality that she appreciates in the honoree. For example, "Grandfather, you are my model of honesty and compassion. Happy Birthday!" You may wish to recall a treasured memory: "You are the most patient grandmother who has ever lived;

I would have failed algebra without you!" The sentiments need not be long, just heartfelt and personal. Present the book as a group on the honoree's birthday. It is sure to be a most treasured gift.

When Louise's godmother turned eighty, she took part in a "card shower" coordinated by her godmother's daughter. Each person wrote a heartfelt sentiment on a blank card and sent it to the daughter, who created a master scrapbook of all the cards. If distance is a challenge, this is a good option.

A Retirement Autograph Book

Yours till Niagara falls.
—Anonymous

Recently, I came across a wonderful bit of memorabilia—my aunt Katherine's autograph book. In her time, autograph books were precious keepsakes that gathered quotes, rhymes, and good wishes of trusted friends and family over a period of time.

Her book includes entries from 1917 through 1940, tracing her life from World War I to her distinguished career as one of the first operating room nurses in the country during the early years of anesthesia. My favorite entry is a John Ruskin quote written to her by Sister Anna Ebert of Lankenau Hospital in Wynnewood, Pennsylvania: "When love and skill work together, expect a masterpiece."

As I read the carefully considered words of so many people who had loved and respected my aunt, I thought about how wonderful it would be to create such a keepsake today as a retirement gift for a special person whose work or character is noteworthy and who remembers this elegant, old-fashioned custom. —V.L.

What You Need

- A good-quality autograph book
- The names and addresses of colleagues and close friends of the elder
- A response form
- Three to six months' time

What You Do

First, buy an attractive, hard-covered gift book, ideally one of the old-fashioned ones that are small and distinctive. If you can't find one like this, there are many small scrapbook or journal-style books available in stationery stores.

Find a way to get the Christmas card list, Rolodex, or address book of the person to be honored. Write to the key people (you may need help from the honoree or another relative), and enclose a simple return form and a self-addressed, stamped envelope.

On the form, draw a box sized to fit the pages of the autograph book. Ask each person to write in ink a short but very personal message to the honoree in the space given (entries of two to six lines; rhymes are great!) and to sign and return it as quickly as possible. Give the deadline as one month before the date you wish to present the book. When you have received the entries, cut out the boxes and paste them into the book to be presented at retirement as a gift from colleagues and close friends.

Honoring a Mentor

We are all in the gutter, but some of us are looking at the stars.

—Oscar Wilde

I have a true stargazer friend. In the midst of a divorce, she planted a magnificent garden, tending her weeping cherry tree, apricot tulips, and the tender grasses between rocks. She would go out at midnight, with a special lamp on an extension cord, to garden under the night sky.

When Dean and I married, Judy brought lemons she had grown that were still attached to the stem. These lemons and Louise's wedding poem were my most memorable wedding gifts.

Sometime later, when I grew my first lemon, I took it to Judy in a spirit of triumph. I am no gardener. She was just as pleased with the significance of that first lemon as I was.

We all have someone who has taught us something special about life, someone who has offered us a new view of our possibilities and of ourselves. This is a ritual to honor such a person. —V.L.

What You Need

- An item such as a plant, tree, quilt, or poem that symbolizes the lesson learned

What You Do

Some day when you have done something well, think about how you learned to do it. Whether you have grown an especially beautiful lemon, baked brownies beyond description, produced your first children's play, or climbed a mountain, someone has inspired you—someone who would love to know of your success. Visit your mentor and take along a symbol of your accomplishment. The greatest gift you can give a teacher is understanding the lesson!

The Accomplishment Book

Things won are done;
joy's soul lies in the doing.
—William Shakespeare

An art student who won a contest, a developmentally disabled child in the Special Olympics, and a Rhodes Scholar all receive awards. Sometimes, awards are given for participation in an event because not everyone wins. Awards elicit pride and self-esteem. One girl may get trophies for winning soccer games and another for a beautiful butterfly collection.

Richard DeFoe, who works at my husband's senior citizens' center, is developmentally disabled and has built his whole life around the Special Olympics. He has won many trophies for track. The awards he has received add immeasurable joy to his life.

Accomplishments never end, whether they are visiting a sick friend, volunteering for a church committee, or taking a niece out to lunch. Expanding the definition of *accomplishment* will help everyone view the world differently.

Many awards get lost when people move. Here is a way to keep the memory of accomplishments in a book that can become a keepsake. —L.N.

What You Need

- A large scrapbook
- A camera

What You Do

When your child wins an award certificate, date one page of the scrapbook and put it there right away. If your child does something special in the house (like paint a room), photograph her doing the activity and place the photo in the book. Fill the book with records of accomplishments for each year, making sure to expand your view of an accomplishment to include not only a good report card or a trophy but things as simple as a child making dinner for the first time.

This book will be a prized possession for her to look over and, when she is feeling down, will help her to see how much she has accomplished. It also will help a child to know that you appreciate not only what society expects of her but also the special ways she expresses her love and personality around the house.

You can also keep an accomplishment book for an older adult who might think, "I don't do anything anymore."

Transitions

We are always in transition. Nothing ever has the tidy beginning or end we like to imagine. The minute we think we have captured something, it is no longer ours; the chrysalis becomes the butterfly, the fire turns to ash.

Somewhere along the way, we learned to dread transition and change. But it doesn't have to be that way. When we can see the transitional state as an ideal situation—in which we are free to exceed prior limits and assumptions—our lives can be enriched beyond our wildest expectations. Transition times offer us the chance to learn flexibility and grace, like the willow bending in the wind.

The Life Collage

If you want to sing out, sing out
And if you want to be free, be free.
—*Cat Stevens*

Many of us see life as a collage, a kaleidoscope of images. Where do we fit in the picture? Where are we going? In collage workshops, participants create pictures of their desires through images and words, focusing on what they want in different areas of their lives: love, travel, money.

In her book *Creative Visualization,* Shakti Gawain shows how mentally picturing what you desire can allow it to appear in your life. Creating a collage is a concrete and creative way of envisioning a reality that you may be stepping into at any moment. The successes of this type of envisioning have been myriad. Some examples include a friend who found the exact apartment she pictured in San Francisco and an older woman who had been single for many years but found a mate within six months of creating her collage.

Perhaps the consciousness-raising that goes with this exercise can allow dreams to come true. Along with becoming aware of what you wish for, let the childhood thrill of cutting and pasting yield to adventures you may never have imagined. —L.N.

What You Need

- Magazines about nature, women's issues, sports, and art
- Sturdy paper or poster board
- Scissors and glue sticks
- Pens
- Other objects if you wish, such as buttons, ribbons, or shells

What You Do

Plan collage time. Gather together as many magazines as you can that contain a variety of images and words. Before you start, focus on your desires. A new home? More money? A mate? More travel? More time alone? More ways to help the world?

You can divide the collage into different areas. For instance, money can be illustrated in one area, where you might paste your income goals for next year; another corner can be about love, showing two people holding hands across a table; another corner can display images of travel, perhaps a ship on its way to Alaska.

You can also cut out words, prayers, poems, or messages—or write your own words in between the pictures. Always put a picture of yourself in the collage. Many people place themselves in the middle of the collage, with the images surrounding them.

If you are not sure of a focus, cut out images that appeal to you and see what kind of picture emerges. For a more 3-D effect, paste the buttons, ribbons, or shells onto the collage. Be as varied as you wish.

Display the collage prominently in your home so you and others who love you can see what you envision. Who knows, it may also qualify as an objet d'art.

When a Friend Moves Away

What has been plaited cannot be unplaited—
Only the strands grow richer with each loss.
                                        —May Sarton

When I was growing up, we moved five times as the Ford Motor Company transferred my father from plant to plant. Each time, I had to say goodbye to friends, knowing I would probably never see them again.

This was sad and confusing for me and left me with the belief that people you come to love go away. Now, many years later, I can see how painful it was for my brother and parents, too, and how much our family needed rituals to make these transitions more gracefully. Here is one simple way to weave a happy memory with another family. —V.L.

What You Need

- Colored ribbons at least one inch wide
- An indelible marker
- Cardboard

What You Do

Ask the members of the family that is moving to recall happy memories of times shared with the family staying behind, and then write them on ribbons. One might read, "I will always remember the Christmas when Anna thought Santa got stuck in the chimney." Ask the other family to do the same.

Weave the ribbons together like a lattice pie crust, using the cardboard as a backing. Present them to the departing family at a farewell dinner. If you like, make two weavings so each family can have one.

Hang the weaving where all family members can see it and be reminded that friendship does not end with distance. Remember to call and write often, especially in the first year away.

Making Choices

Life does not give itself to one who tries to keep all its advantages at once. I have often thought morality may perhaps consist solely in the courage of making a choice.
—Léon Blum

My younger daughter, an avid soccer player, recently decided to switch from a highly competitive team to a recreational team. The month prior to the change and the day of the decision were not easy. We all had many feelings about the situation, but in the end it was her decision. I thought of how she could best let go of the old team and adjust to the new one without losing her self-esteem and enthusiasm for soccer.

Changing schools, teams, or households, can be very difficult for a child. It is important to acknowledge the child's feelings and help her work through painful memories rather than suppress them. —L.N.

What You Need

- Your child's favorite cake with icing and two candles
- The parents or family and friends most important to the child

What You Do

After a family dinner, give the child some time to talk about the change in her life. Perhaps she wants to say more, even though the decision has already been made. Maybe she feels that someone wronged her or that she has to give up some precious friendships. Let her talk until she is finished, ending with her hopes for the new team or school.

Ask your child to light two candles, close together. As she lights the first candle, let her say, "I'm leaving my old team and, though I may miss some friends, I know that I have made the right choice for me. I wish the team all the best, as I wish myself all the best!"

Next, ask your child to light the second candle and say, "I move to my new team, with the love of my family and friends. I trust myself completely and I made a good decision!" Then, ask your child to blow out both candles and serve the cake to the guests. Change can be delicious!

Welcoming a Young Woman into the Circle

You bring me back where old women dress me in satin, let me sing with lips of red wind.

—Louise Nayer

My sister Anne lives in the Virgin Islands and talks about a special spot on Hull Bay, a sand crescent between two green points jutting into the Atlantic Ocean. Rocky coral reefs visible as dark blotches mark the otherwise breathtakingly turquoise sea dotted with fishing boats.

One night, under a full moon, a group of women met on Hull Bay to honor a twelve-year-old they had known for many years, celebrating her transition from a girl to a young woman. Though most of us don't live in paradise, full moons exist all over the world. Here is a ritual to help a girl feel proud of growing into womanhood and feel connected to a community of women she can turn to during the pivotal years of adolescence. —L.N.

What You Need

- A group of women gathered under a full moon
- A small gift from nature
- A leather pouch or small purse
- Food and drink brought by everyone

What You Do

Form a circle around the girl and ask each person to speak to her, recounting memories from when she was an infant to the young woman she is now. Each woman can also speak of the transition to womanhood in her own life, as a way of supporting her through this change.

Next, each woman speaks of her hopes for the young person and walks to the middle of the circle to give her a hug and present her with a small gift from nature, such as a piece of coral or a seashell that can be put into a small pouch and kept in a special place.

When the ceremony is over, eat and drink together. If you are fortunate enough to live in the Virgin Islands, you can then swim in warm waters under the full moon! End the evening with a blessing:

> We wish you courage to stand up for yourself,
> intelligence to make good choices,
> strength to pursue your goals

and more than enough love surrounding you
as you go on this new journey and adventure.
Call on us at any time.

A Father-and-Son Journey

*Thou wilt shew me the path of life; in thy presence is the
fullness of joy.*

—*Psalm 16:11*

When a boy reaches his teenage years, the balance of power between
him and his father begins to shift. The son may run faster than his
dad or throw a ball farther or more easily reach a high cabinet.

When a son turns thirteen, a dad who likes camping can take
his son on an expedition, setting this time aside to teach some
of the skills he has learned over the years, passing the torch of
manhood and creating a special time for them. —L.N.

What You Need

- Camping gear, including a compass and water purification
  system
- A campsite with fire ring
- Two walking sticks found in nature
- Carving tools
- A present from dad to son

What You Do

You and your son should plan the trip together, but you choose the trail and camping site. The young man must complete a list of essentials for the adventure—from the amount of drinking water needed to the renting of a bear-proof container (if you're in bear country!) to a list of food and other necessities.

Before or during the trip, show your son how to use the compass and water purification system, survival skills that are now passed down. The first evening away, when night falls, build a simple pyramid-style fire together, letting the younger man start the fire as a symbol of his growing manhood.

The next day, on a hike, each of you can choose a walking stick from the brush. That evening, carve your initials and significant images into your sticks.

As you carve, discuss what has been important to you throughout your life and given you strength. Then, point out the strengths you see in your son, giving him confidence that his father believes in him as he enters the teen years.

You may then choose to give your son something passed down from previous generations, such as an arm patch, a medal, or a pocketknife.

When you return home, leave your walking sticks near the front door as a symbol of your commitment to spend time together and to continue to talk about what is important to you.

The Letter Shower for a Teen

Ask the questions now; then someday quietly, without noticing it you will live some distant day into the answer.
—Rainer Maria Rilke

The teenage years are ones of transition from childhood to adulthood. Have you ever seen a young adult holding a favorite stuffed animal while waiting to go to a rock concert? The night before Sarah started high school, she crawled into bed with me for a few minutes. We both knew what was going on and just held each other.

At our Unitarian Universalist congregation, Sarah took part in a coming-of-age ceremony, but we wanted to do something at home, too. We decided to create a book of letters from those who love her as well as a work of art that she could treasure.

I found some artwork representative of the teenage transition time—three concentric circles of images: a butterfly in the middle, dragons in the next circle, and angels in the outer circle. Sarah was moving from girlhood into a larger world, transforming like the butterfly and protected by the angels. —L.N.

What You Need

- Letters from relatives and adult friends of your child
- A scrapbook with a decorative and personalized cover
- Important pictures that represent different stages in your child's life
- A work of art that speaks to the experience of a thirteen year old

What You Do

Ask relatives and friends to write a letter to your child when she turns thirteen. Tell them the letter needs to be sent by a particular date. They could write to the child about her strengths, her courage, her talents, and how they trust that she will become a wonderful adult. Remember the special moments of childhood and offer words of wisdom, without preaching.

Sarah's dad wrote in part of his letter, "I see you not only as a beautiful, intelligent, talented, and strong young woman, but as a soulful traveler on this earth, a daughter I deeply love." Later, he wrote, "Find the path that is truly your own." Whatever you write, write it from the heart.

Collect the letters in a scrapbook, interspersing them with pictures representing milestone events in your child's life. Have a special dinner with some of the most important people in your child's life. Light candles, bring out a cake, and present the book. Bring a positive perspective to the newfound freedom and independence that your child has begun to experience.

Along with the book, give her a painting that best expresses the transitional nature of the teenage years. She will most likely want to hang it up in her room. If that is not the case, let her choose where she wants to display it.

Laying Aside a Child's Love Object

Little bear, little bear,
how I take you everywhere.
You are all the world to me,
friend and toy and family.
You may be smelly, torn and stained,
but with you I am not afraid.
—Virginia Lang

I have a terrible memory of losing my childhood blanket. The day my mother decided I should be done with it, she told me she was just going to wash it, but it never came back from the wash. Anyone who thinks this is no big deal to a child is dead wrong. I can still remember every detail about that exchange and the look on her face that said something really big was going down!

So when we mistakenly left YuWen's beloved stuffed camel on an airplane, I was devastated. How could I ever explain that "Jim" was gone? I made up an elaborate story about how he had stayed on the plane because it was going on to Paris and he wanted to see the Eiffel Tower. When her godfather went to Europe, he sent her a postcard from Jim and a drawing of the camel wearing a beret, sitting in a café near the Eiffel Tower—looking at a framed picture of YuWen that he had taken along! —V.L.

What You Need

- A special moment to celebrate your child's beloved object

What You Do

Once your child has outgrown her need to have her "Jim" as a daily appendage, take a moment together to preserve it so that she can see the importance you are giving him. Ask her what she thinks he would like. She may wish to place him in a satin-lined bed or in a shadowbox that can be hung. She may be happy simply making a special place for him on a bedroom shelf. Let her say words from her heart as you give him a place of honor.

Fortunately, YuWen found a new love after Jim—a bear named Albert who she wraps in a carefully chosen tea towel when it rains. What happens to Albert matters to her . . . and I still want my blanket back!

A Celebratory Haircut

Fair tresses man's imperial race ensnare.
And beauty draws us with a single hair.
—Alexander Pope

What is it about hair? In the Bible, Samson is tamed when Delilah cuts his hair. According to some Eastern traditions, the hair on our heads lies on the crown chakra—the energy center that connects us to the community and the cosmos. In Western religions, you often see pictures of angels with halos in roughly the same place as the crown chakra. Perhaps that is why cutting hair has so much power for us and carries such symbolic meaning.

In Peru, I had the opportunity to cut the hair of a young girl named Brigida. My traveling group participated in her coming-of-age ceremony at the base of Ausangate, one of the most sacred mountains in Peru. Each of us was asked to cut a small piece of Brigida's hair from the nape of her neck and place it in a ceremonial bowl. As each of us took the scissors, we called her by name and gently stroked her head. Those of us who spoke Spanish whispered words of love and support.

Afterward, we shared a celebratory meal of potatoes and roasted guinea pig and gave small gifts of money to Brigida. I will always remember the look on her face as we crossed into her world, her time, and her Andean home through this simple ritual. While ritual haircutting is not observed in our culture, it may be meaningful as part of a coming-of-age ceremony for a young girl who has made the decision to cut off long hair. —V.L.

What You Need

- Family and special friends
- A decorative bowl
- Scissors
- A hairdresser
- The address of Locks of Love

What You Do

Sit in a circle and place a beautiful bowl in its center. Beginning with parents and grandparents, ask each member present to cut a small piece of hair from the nape of the child's neck, calling the child by name and speaking a private message of love and support in her ear.

Place each lock of hair in the bowl. Pass the scissors from person to person until everyone has had a turn. When the circle is complete, join hands and spend a few minutes in silence. You may want to give small gifts of money or attractive hair ornaments for the child's new look.

Ask your hairdresser to join you, or make an appointment for her to cut the hair professionally in the salon later that day. Send the clipped hair to Locks of Love, an organization that makes wigs for ill children. Be sure to contact them for detailed instructions before you cut. You may reach them at Locks of Love, 2925 10th Ave. North, Suite 102, Lakeworth, FL 33461; (888) 896-1588.

Keeping Faith with a
Newly Disabled Friend

I thank God for my handicaps, for through them, I have found myself, my work, and my God.

—Helen Keller

I learned recently of a men's group that meets every week at the home of a newly paralyzed man whose name is Joe. After his injury, Joe fell into a deep depression. His despair began to have severe consequences for his family.

The men's group gathers once a week at his home to go out for a lunch date. Joe chooses whom he wants to ride with that day. His spirits have markedly improved because of this weekly ritual.

When I heard Joe's story, I realized that I had been holding back from meeting my new neighbor who is bedridden. Her husband and son, who care for her, told me that most of her friends have fallen away since her illness. Even her sister doesn't come around. Why is it so hard to look suffering in the eye?

A Chinese expression advises, "To have a friend is to love the crows on his roof." When misfortune comes to people we love, we need to learn to love their crows. —V.L.

What You Need

- Two to three hours, once a week

What You Do

Organize a group event that your friend can enjoy. Think about preparing your car for his comfort and making certain the restaurant, movie theater, or home you choose to visit is accessible and easy to navigate.

If the person is bedridden, take a picnic to his room each week with real napkins and fresh flowers. Bring a book he would enjoy, and take turns reading out loud and discussing it as if in a book club. Or become a writing group, sharing feelings through words. The beginning of my writing life began in a writing group of four that met in Louise's bedroom once a week. That group grew to eight and met for over eight years.

From Couple to Parents

Today we are three; what happened to you and me?
—Virginia Lang

One of the greatest challenges for a couple who decides to have a child is making the transition from lovers and friends to lovers and parents. The arrival of a newborn begins a profound shift in the parents' relationship, as both partners find their way toward a new understanding of themselves.

While there is delight and awe in the process of redefinition, there is also a loss of place. For a while at least, the parents' new roles can seem like bit parts in the high drama of the newborn, who now takes center stage. Conscious recognition of this fundamental shift from couple to family may help to ease the transition.

What You Need

- Quiet time to be together as a couple, close to the time of birth
- Two pencils and paper

What You Do

Express to each other your hopes for your family's future. You might write down your thoughts and offer them to each other, or you may write a statement of hope as a couple, such as the one that follows.

A Statement of Our Hopes as New Parents

As our marriage blossoms with the new life entrusted to
   us, we hope:
To respect and deepen the love that brought us together
To fall in love with our child, while we keep our love
   alive
To make time for each other, to listen, to play, to just be
To move into our new roles as parents with humor and
   acceptance
To support each other with understanding and compas-
   sion
To acknowledge the loss of freedom with largeness of
   spirit
To draw on the support of family and friends, while
   finding our own way to parent

Type up and frame your statement of hope and place it where you can be reminded of it.

When You Don't Get Your Dream Job

Disappointment is often the salt of life.
—Theodore Parker

Some time ago, my husband was a hair's breadth away from a dream job—the one he never imagined would materialize. After five trips and more than twenty interviews, the job was offered to someone else. Unfortunately, there was no consolation prize.

After a few weeks of intense anger followed by deep sadness, he began to see that he had learned something from the experience that he would apply to the next opportunity. Together, we talked it over, realizing that this kind of loss also needs a process for the anger and frustration to subside and new possibilities to emerge. —V.L.

What You Need

- A time and place to be alone with your most trusted friend, spouse, partner, or mentor
- Two hours
- A pad and pencil

What You Do

Seat yourselves comfortably in a place where you will not be disturbed. Make sure no phones or faxes will interfere, and give yourselves two hours, minimum, for this two-part ritual.

Ask your friend, spouse, partner, or mentor to use the pad and pencil to take notes while you speak freely, allowing any and all feelings to emerge unedited and uncensored. The friend can ask these or similar questions:

1. What went wrong?
2. Was it avoidable?
3. Did you get a poor reference? Can you talk to that person?
4. Was there a stronger candidate; do you feel you screwed up?
5. Are you left feeling unfinished because you never really found out what happened?
6. Is there any gracious high road left to take—a letter expressing future interest, a thank-you for the opportunity to interview?
7. Was there an injustice that warrants legal action?
8. Was the process too long, unfair, demeaning?
9. Was the job misrepresented?
10. Are you well-suited for this work, job, or process? Do you want another shot?

When you have exhausted these thoughts, take a break and walk around a bit to clear your head.

Return to your places. With your friend continuing to write down key words, brainstorm all the positive aspects of the opportunity. No matter how silly, just blurt things out, such as, "I would've gotten an office with a window!" or "The promotional possibilities were unlimited." Continue until you have identified all the things you wanted from the position and will want from the next one.

When you feel finished, listen to the list of comments read back to you. Then, using the list, make a statement out loud, like this one: "I intend to find an even better position that offers me promotional possibilities, terrific colleagues, generous benefits," and so on. Fill in the blanks with the wish list. Provide a date by which you'd like to find this position.

Express thanks for any lessons learned from the experience and be sure to thank your friend for her thoughtful listening. Close the door softly on this episode, keeping in mind that burning bridges may not help. The same company or opportunity may come up again. Let hope begin to replace your anger, and ask your unconscious to go to work on attracting an even better opportunity for you.

Creating the Home You Want

Come here. Sit beside your childhood.
Drink from the old words.
You will find your own clock.
Listen, it's your heart.

—*Louise Nayer*

In our twenties, thirties, and sometimes later, many of us drift between relationships, jobs, and places to live. All too often, we wake up from this constant drifting to realize we are not "home."

At twenty-four, after finishing graduate school in Buffalo, I packed all my belongings in a 1968 Camaro and drove across the country alone. I called my parents from a phone booth in the middle of Colorado while watching the hawks circle the sky and chickens run in circles in a nearby yard. I tried hard to be free of the past. Years later, I wanted the opposite—to create a home. —L.N.

What You Need

- Two pieces of paper
- Pens or pencils

What You Do

On a sheet of paper, write the word *home* in the middle of the page and draw a circle around it. Write down any words you associate with your childhood home on tentacles coming out of the circle. The words might reflect where you lived, the noise, the people, difficulties, joys, sorrows. You might use words such as *noisy, music, alcohol, brother, moving*. Under each word, you can write more about the noise, the music, and so on. You probably will have a wide range of memories from early childhood to high school. If this exercise brings up too many bad feelings, make sure to have a good friend or counselor to work with you.

On a second sheet of paper, a day or two later, make another circle with tentacles and write down what you would like in your new home. What would be different? Was your childhood house noisy and would you like more silence? Was your childhood home lonely and would you like more people at the dinner table? Write down whatever comes to mind, using as much detail as possible.

Put away your first "map" and place your new "home" on the refrigerator. Look at it often, reminding yourself of what you want.

Nighttime City Walks

Boys came bearing cornstalk violins
And they rubbed the cornstalk bows with resins
And the three sat there scraping of their joy.
—Galway Kinnell

A few years before my husband turned fifty, he began to take night walks in the city with his good friend Brad and a few other men. The walks symbolized a desire to take to the streets. At midnight, when they climbed above the cover of fog on Twin Peaks, they always encountered the ever-changing view of San Francisco at night.

The group scaled San Francisco hills from Mount Davidson to Twin Peaks, sometimes climbing for three hours, coming home exhausted and exhilarated. They explored the city as they had as young boys, with skinned knees and stories to tell. —L.N.

What You Need

- Water and snacks
- A flashlight
- Maps of the city
- A first-aid kit
- Reflectors on your clothing
- A knapsack
- A cell phone (just in case)

What You Do

Plan your city adventure with your friends, deciding how far the group can realistically walk and agreeing to push a little past one another's comfort zone. Take food and drink, a flashlight, and other necessities. Make safety a priority.

Have fun just being together on an adventure, the type you remember from childhood treasure hunts and days of just going out in the woods to play. Let all money and family cares drift away for the evening as you enjoy time with your buddies.

If there is time when the hike is over, go out for a drink and recount stories of the adventure. My husband and his friends have had many stories to tell—discovering blackberry brambles near the University of California Medical Center, catching poison oak, and calling the fire department to rescue a cat trapped in a sewer. Each adventure was new and exciting.

A Woman's Midlife Journey

In a dream you are never 80.
—Anne Sexton

The minute we hang on to something, it begins to change. Love changes, children change, our work changes, our bodies change. In this culture, we often resist change, anesthetizing ourselves with shopping or food, alcohol or drugs, escapes of a thousand natures—anything to keep the illusion of control.

Lately, my menopausal body has been knocking me about, trying to get my attention. I haven't wanted to listen, to admit that a profound change is occurring and that I am becoming a different person in many ways. I have come to see that the energy expended in resisting this transition would be far better directed toward self-acceptance and humor, if I am to grow older gracefully and happily. —V.L.

What You Need

- Time alone once a week for as long as it takes
- A journal
- A litany of acceptance
- A recent photo of yourself

What You Do

As you begin to notice your changing body, spend some time alone every week with a journal. Write about your body, your mind, the changes you are experiencing, and how you feel about them. Compose personal affirmations of self-acceptance or use the words of these:

Affirmations of Acceptance

It is time to please myself.

It is time to treat the life-giving powers of my body with gentleness.

It is time to allow the creative power within me to find new expression.

It is time to open my heart in self-acceptance so I may love and serve others and myself with all I have learned.

It is time to step into the middle of my life grateful for the wisdom, grace, and courage I now possess.

During this time, take a thoughtful look at yourself. Frame a recent picture of yourself and place it where you can appreciate what you look like now. You may want to adopt some of the following new practices.

- Consider a change of image. Buy clothes with simpler lines and of better quality. If you wear perfume, find a new, more complex scent. Maybe you'd like to grow your hair impractically long or change your look in some other way that expresses who you are now. If you have trouble doing this alone, plan a "menopause makeover" in a spa or retreat setting where you can create a treasured memory with a few close women friends over fine aged wine.

- Try a new physical activity. Perhaps you would enjoy yoga, swimming, or jogging. If you don't like exercise, at least plan to take a good walk each day.

- If you are tired of cooking, try eating out or preparing simpler meals instead of cooking so often. Simplify daily tasks that rob you of creative time. Clean less, paint or write more.

- Organize a small women's group for support and friendship. Learn to meditate as a group, and enjoy the peace and respite of your own good company.

- Find a younger woman to mentor, either in her career or in her personal life.
- If you are a camper or would like a more rugged rite of passage, consider going on a Vision Quest, a solo wilderness experience to get in touch with yourself and help redefine your goals.

Losing a Job

If we had no winter, the spring would not be so pleasant: if we did not sometimes taste of adversity, prosperity would not be so welcome.

—Anne Bradstreet

The workplace today often consists of huge mergers, corporate downsizings, and profound displacements. Many hard-working people who have been loyal to their employers have found that loyalty means little when a company is sold to a conglomerate. Manual laborers without technical skills are sidelined in the new information economy.

As the sweeping ebbs and flows of global economics wash over us, it is easy to feel powerless and abandoned. This is the very time when friends, family, and ritual matter most.

What You Need

- Close friends and family members
- A circle of chairs

What You Do

Gather trusted friends and family members who understand what the unemployed person is going through. Choose only those who will be not be judgmental.

Arrange a circle of chairs or pillows. When everyone has been seated, the person who lost the job should speak first, thanking the group for their support and relating the facts of the lost job.

Each person should then ask whatever questions she may have and offer whatever help is appropriate. A parent may offer temporary financial help, a best friend may offer child care during the job search, someone else may know of a contact or even another job offer.

Each member should call the unemployed person weekly until he finds another job, offering moral and practical support for as long as the search takes.

The End of a Marriage

I never hated a man enough to give him diamonds back.
—Zsa Zsa Gabor

No single moment embraces the dissolution of a couple quite like the day when the rings come off. You want to do something with the rings—but what?

What You Need

- The ring

What You Do

We asked a bunch of people what they did to mark the moment the rings came off and how they dealt with it afterward. Here are the best ideas. Feel free to choose one or come up with your own based on any of these.

- "My mom crafted her rings into a gold pendant in a jewelry-making class. She cut the rings, flattened them, rounded the pieces, and placed them side-by-side in an offset vertical design. To finish the pendant, she had a goldsmith professionally set the diamond into the design. The people at the class cheered her on, yelling, 'Go, Elizabeth!' as she cut the rings. It was definitely a powerful moment in her life. I imagine her tiny five-foot-one-inch frame at some sort of power saw, with massive goggles on and sparks flying!"

- "I returned my ring to my husband with a letter that explained how I felt about the twenty-eight years we'd had together and what I hoped to achieve without him."

- "I knew someone who had it melted down, with other jewelry her ex gave her, into a nugget that she wears on her charm bracelet. The act of melting it down was closure for her."

- "I threw mine in a cup with old screws and other odds and ends in the kitchen junk drawer. Every two years or so, I find it when I'm looking for something else. That's the moment of ceremony. It's the tiny epiphany—more of a reminder—that I've moved on successfully."

- "I have a friend whose parents split when she was a teenager. Her mom gave her wedding ring to her and her engagement ring to her sister as keepsakes. It meant a lot to my friend because it was a way for her to hold on to the times when her parents were happily married."

Honoring a Special Elder

A teacher affects eternity; he can never tell where his influence stops.

—Henry Brooks Adams

A few weeks before my uncle Bush died, we gathered at our family farm where he had spent many happy hours. Mowing the meadow was always his special love, and he spent hundreds of hours on the tractor in communion with the land. After mowing, he would go in the house, take off his yellow straw hat, and ask my mom for a big glass of ice tea.

At this last gathering, he brought his work shoes, as he had so many times before. Though he hasn't mowed in a decade, he still came ready to work, at ninety-one years old. All afternoon as he and I sat and watched my husband and brother mow, he kept turning to me and commenting, "They really like it, don't they?" I knew then that he had what he needed to let go of this life: the sight of the next generation caring happily for his beloved farm.

I felt so glad that he had had this final satisfaction and could leave his life having passed the torch. He died peacefully in his sleep five weeks later. —V.L.

What You Need

- Special time together

What You Do

Invite the elder to watch a younger member of the family perform something the elder loved to do—perhaps a grandson can cook an old family recipe, a daughter can tune up the car, a niece can sew or knit.

If there is a specific task the elder performed for the family but can no longer manage, such as carving the turkey on Thanksgiving, ask him to teach his technique to a younger member; or if he has already done so, let him watch his student perform. Though the task or skill may be as simple as mowing grass, it may hold great significance for him.

Saying Goodbye to a Home

Barn's burnt down—now I can see the moon.
—Masahide

When my aunt Margaret and uncle Albert sold their home, I think I was more upset than they were. This simple red brick home was the place of many happy family gatherings, a place I always felt safe and deeply loved.

I knew it was time for Aunt Margaret and Uncle Albert to simplify, yet all I could think about was how I would miss the crunch of their green metal rockers, the smell of their boxwoods, the burgundy-and-turquoise kitchen where many hands had made light labor of washing dishes after a holiday meal. I have never before nor since had so much feeling for a house. It was hard to say goodbye. —V.L.

What You Need

- A day in the house before the packing begins
- A camera
- A candle

What You Do

While things are still in place, photograph every room, capturing the placement of beloved objects and special collections. Be sure to photograph the people who are moving as they sit in their favorite chairs or at their usual spots at the table. Make copies of the prints and keep the photos in two small acid-free albums, one for you and one to give later as a gift.

During the packing, offer to help sort and sift through the memories so you can share one more special memory in the home.

As you leave the house for the last time, take a moment to walk through each room with a small candle in hand and say goodbye to each room. If the family is together, join hands and say, "We are grateful to have shared so many happy moments here."

Retirement

*Age is an opportunity no less
Than youth itself, though in
another dress.
And as the evening twilight
fades away
The sky is filled with stars invisible by day.*
—Henry Wadsworth Longfellow

Some people work until their last breaths, dedicated to their jobs or unable to retire because of finances. For many people, though, retirement offers new opportunities—time to paint or draw again, time to go fly-fishing, or to spend more time with family.

Many people have identified themselves with their jobs so much that they find little pleasure in other activities, mainly because they have had little time or mental space to explore other venues. Those who have avocations, passions for something, do better during retirement.

My husband is director of a senior citizens' center and has seen many people blossom in their later years, becoming painters and sculptors, finding and sometimes reclaiming talents from their childhoods. How do we make the transition smoothly? There is no easy answer, for retirement has to do with health, finances, relationships, and attitude. But this ritual may help people find a new path in life. —L.N.

What You Need

- Twelve index cards and a pen
- A bowl
- Time alone once a month
- A calendar

What You Do

A year before you retire, write down on each index card one avocation that interests you: constructing remote-control boats, drawing, going to gem shows, playing golf, singing in a choir, whatever moves you. On the back of each card, write down the name of one month of the year. Place all the index cards in a bowl.

If your card for January says "constructing remote-control boats," spend some time during that month researching the field, buying magazines related to model boats, visiting hobby shops, and connecting with others who enjoy the same activity.

Make sure to write down the avocations on your kitchen calendar, one for each month of the year. By the time you retire, you will have some idea of which world (or worlds) you wish to enter as a retiree. The preparation will be invaluable. You can leave the workforce certain that many other people will welcome you with open arms.

Helping an Elder Move to Assisted Living

I want to come home to my overstuffed chair, to the smell of baking chocolate, to the purple of lilacs. My heart keeps time by my grandfather clock. Can you hear it now?
—Margaret Bauer

When my aunt Margaret moved from her home to assisted living, she found the transition difficult. Though people in her new home were kind and the place was attractive, the loss of freedom was very unsettling to her. Meals were prepared, beds made, prescriptions delivered all without any input from her. She came to feel she was simply not needed in her own life.

To make matters worse, during the move she had been too ill to oversee the placement of her possessions. Often, when I visited, she would ask me where her rocking chair had gone or "Will Johnny get the grandfather clock?" Moving to a hotel-like atmosphere robbed her of her sense of identity and control. Her objects, though not important in themselves, took on symbolic importance. —V.L.

What You Need

- A camera
- Special items such as favorite furniture, special jewelry, and tableware
- A small photo album
- A pen
- Handmade items from children, artwork, trophies, and special cards

What You Do

Photograph all the best-loved furniture and treasured items that will not accompany the person into assisted living. Place them in a special photo album and write under each picture where that item has gone. If possible, photograph each item in its new location with the grandchild, son, daughter, or friend who is now enjoying it. You might choose to put a large-type caption underneath each picture with a thank-you quote from each recipient.

When you visit your elder at the assisted-living home, make it a point to talk about how much the item is appreciated and make it a ritual to look at the album together, remembering happy times in the past. Let the children present their handiwork to the elder.

Caring for Future Generations

Tread softly on this shallow earth,
the dust is blowing in eyes that don't see
the oceans are gathering in floods of despair,
the earth quakes angrily.

—Virginia Lang

What will your great-great-great-granddaughter be doing? Where will she live? In an overpopulated city? On another planet? What will she wear? Chinese silk, a detox uniform, a space suit? What will she eat? Food? Nutrient powder? What will she be like? Cloned? Genetically perfect?

Do these questions sound like science fiction? Have you thought about life in the third millennium, and if not, why do you think you haven't?

Native American families looked seven generations into the future in their thinking and decision making. They thought about how their actions in the present would affect the next seven generations to come. In our rush to get what we think is rightfully ours, we seldom act as if there will be any future generations at all.

We consume and discard with abandon, unwilling to look at our dying planet and the sicknesses of mind and body that are endemic to our consumerism. How would we live if we really cared about future generations and thought about their well-being?

What You Need

- A weekend alone with your spouse once a year
- A pencil and paper
- A tape recorder

What You Do

Picture your great-great-great-grandchildren in a third-millennium lifestyle. Consider what they will need that may no longer be available on the earth. Think about what you are doing today that may be undermining their future.

Decide how you want to use the resources and time available to you now. This could mean anything from limiting your family size to using and advocating solar energy to working for an effective recycling program in your community to creating a new educational model for your children. Start by addressing questions like these:

- What do we know about the world's population, and how does that relate to our plans for the size of our family?
- What do we know about efforts in our community to safeguard precious wildlife, wetlands, or beaches? How can we help?
- What are our children learning that will equip them for the pace of technological change? Are they creative enough for the next century? Are they getting what they need from our school system?

- What are we buying that is destructive to the earth? Are we supporting companies whose values we respect? How do we treat animals and other species that have no voice?

- Where do our investment dollars go? Do we know enough about the industries and charities we support?

Make two lists, one of short-term strategies such as recycling or eating more organic food, the second of plans with more far-reaching consequences, such as limiting family size. Tape-record your commitments. Play it on the same day the next year to gauge your success, and update your family's commitment as you learn more.

Some ecologists think it is already too late to save the earth. But we can prove them wrong. Vow to inform yourself and to bring consciousness, compassion, and seven-generation thinking to every new decision your family makes. We're running out of time.

Loss

To live a full life is to experience many small deaths, to tumble out of the comfortable nest of our expectations, to learn about grief. When we find the courage to meet life head-on, the loss of a family member, loss of a friend, loss of health, or loss of youth can all be our teachers, the ways we learn the meaning of compassion.

The pain of loss forces us to think, to discover, and to seek out others, drawing them to us in new and intimate ways. Loss is an entryway to new understandings, an invitation to explore the rain-soaked, rutted roads of our lives, and a reminder to cherish times of comfort and joy.

How to Bury a Goldfish

Even in the smallest things, we express who we are.
—Virginia Lang

If you have a child who has lost a pet, you know how difficult it is to talk about death. Did you say too much or not enough? When YuWen was two, she lost a goldfish because her well-intentioned mother overfed it.

As I contemplated the usual trip to the toilet, I thought about what a horrible message I was sending. This precious thing that had contained life and had meant so much to her was about to get the same treatment as her digested dinner! I chose instead a simple backyard burial, with a role for YuWen to play. —V.L.

What You Need

- A gardening glove
- A small plot of ground
- A trowel or a shovel
- A flower
- A calendar and pen

What You Do

Ask your child to see for herself that the fish is no longer breathing and has no further need for her care. If it feels right, have her gently hold the fish in her hand (using the glove, if you prefer) and carry it outside to a small plot in the garden or near a tree. Dig a small hole and let her place the fish in it.

Hold your child's hand and say with her, "We will miss you and we're glad you came to live with us." Then, gently cover the fish with soil. YuWen likes to sing, so she made up a song for the fish.

Finally, place a flower on the spot and visit the site once or twice in the next week or so. You may want to place a special stone or a small marker made by the child on the site. Circle the date of the death on the calendar to indicate its importance.

For a beloved family pet like a dog or cat, you may wish to wrap the animal in a soft cloth and choose a designated animal burial space in your yard, or have the animal cremated and scatter the ashes in a place that is special to the family, such as a lake or a flower garden.

You may also wish to set up a "memory table" or mantle display with a happy picture of the pet including a few special objects such as a favorite chew toy or leash. Set a small votive candle next to the picture and light it for a week or two to signify the importance of the pet's loss to the family.

When a Child Loses a Parent

When I get to the farm, I open every drawer;
I look in the breakfront where she kept the linens,
Under the yellowed tablecloth with the slate gray roses,
In the whatnot drawer in the funnels and sieves,
In the button box, in the memories of smocked dresses,
In the highboy under blankets with torn bunting,
In the smell of her hankies worn soft with tears.
Where are you mother? Where have you gone?
                                                    —Virginia Lang

When a young child loses a parent, that death reverberates through the rest of the child's life. Some parents who know they are terminally ill can prepare their children for the loss by gathering objects to be saved as cherished mementos, helping parent and child begin to deal with this enormous loss. The keepsake shelf can be anywhere in a child's room or in the closet if the child wants to keep it private.

What You Need

- A tape recorder
- A journal
- Photos
- Cherished objects or clothing
- Perfume or scents

What You Do

If it's possible for the parent to speak into a tape recorder, ask him to speak from the heart and give the child confidence that he will grow up to be a strong person who has been deeply loved and will continue to be loved. This very private tape can be placed on the keepsake shelf and listened to as needed.

Ask the parent to write as much as he can into a journal, lovingly communicating with his child. Ask other adults to find photos of both parent and child in happy times together. Collect the parent's special objects, such as a favorite mug, album, or book, to be kept on the shelf.

Place on this special shelf a bottle of perfume or a scented piece of clothing that reminds the child of the parent's smell. Let the child know that it is normal and perfectly okay to want to be reminded of the smells surrounding the one who loved him so much. Make it clear that the keepsake shelf is personal and that no one may touch it without the child's permission.

Losing an Unborn Child

We are all unformed like the universe with its black holes, its explosions. That some of us leave before being born just means that they reach the stars earlier. Look up. Their lights, tiny stars, bathe us in liquid light.

—Louise Nayer

Losing an unborn child is profoundly saddening. The physical exhaustion and the emotional feeling of loss may persist for months and even years. Many women are afraid to talk about their feelings. Typical responses are often inadvertently insensitive: "You're young, so you have nothing to worry about; you can always have another one" or "Children can be so difficult—enjoy your freedom."

A woman thinks of her unborn child on the anniversary of the due date. How old would the child be? What talents and characteristics would the child have? Here is a ritual that may help a woman who has lost a child before birth begin to accept and integrate the loss in her life.

What You Need

- Friends (her partner and/or one or two close friends)
- Healing hands
- Beautiful music
- Refreshments
- A pen and paper
- A tree

What You Do

Pick a date. It can be significant (the anniversary of the loss or the due date). Ask the woman to lie down on a couch or bed, and ask her partner or close friends to gently lay their hands on her so she is completely relaxed. Play soothing music. Let the woman express whatever she wants to about this particular event in her life—tears, anger, nostalgia, or even the simple joy that the people closest to her are there to acknowledge a part of her that she's kept private.

Then, share a cup of something hot. Designate a speaker to say, "You are holding your baby in your arms. Feel your strength as a mother, how secure you make your child feel. Now, you are singing a song to your baby, your beautiful voice gently rocking your baby to sleep. Feel the love you hold in your heart and your hands, a love without beginning or end."

Then, ask the mother and partner to speak: "We are sorry we will not hold you in our arms, but we will always hold you in our hearts." Ask the parents to name the baby if it's comfortable for them to do so. Let them say the name out loud. Ask them both to close their eyes and hold the baby in their mind's eye. Tell them to call up this moment of love and support anytime they want or need it.

Sometime later within the year, go as a group to plant a tree in honor of the child. If the parents have no yard, you might donate a tree to a public park, a city street, or a special place you like to visit.

Accepting Infertility

You can't say anguish in any
linear way. It comes out in pieces.
—Nancy Shaffer

Many women who want children suffer deeply when they cannot become pregnant. Some choose to pursue an often long and exhausting road of infertility treatment; others allow nature to take its course. Because I lived through this deep disappointment, I know that no amount of support or words of comfort could begin to address my profound feelings of loss until some of my anger was released. —V.L.

What You Need

- Time alone in nature
- The poem "The Song of the Barren Orange Tree"
- A branch
- A journal and pen
- A litany of healing

What You Do

Find a quiet place in nature to be alone. Read silently "The Song of the Barren Orange Tree."

Song of the Barren Orange Tree

Woodcutter.
Cut my shadow from me.
Free me from the torment
of seeing myself without fruit.
Why was I born among mirrors?
The day walks in circles around me,
and the night copies me
in all its stars.
I want to live without seeing myself.
And I will dream that ants
and thistleburrs are my
leaves and my birds.
Woodcutter.
Cut my shadow from me.
Free me from the torment
of seeing myself without fruit.
—Federico García Lorca

Allow yourself to feel all the sadness and rage that is within you. Scream as loud as you like for as long as you like. If it helps, find a branch and break it into many pieces, hitting it on the ground as hard as you can.

When you are exhausted, let yourself cry for as long as you wish. Later that night, write out your feelings in a journal. Before you go to sleep, say these words silently or aloud:

I am whole.
I am well.
I accept myself fully, just as I am.
My nurturing heart is whole and fertile.
I will allow a new self to emerge.
This is not fair.
Life is not fair.
I will go on.

A Ritual for Grief and Loss

In a real dark night of the soul it is always three o'clock in the morning.

—F. Scott Fitzgerald

There are times in life when all we want to do is cry. When my mother died suddenly, I was so shocked and sad, I wandered into Grace Cathedral in San Francisco and just sat and sobbed. A priest walked up to me and sat down, his arm over my shoulder, and asked, "What's wrong, little tiger?"

The tiger is my animal and I have often been likened to one, so it took me aback when this man, who didn't know me at all, saw through my tears to the stronger person within. He talked with me for a long time about the loss of his wife and his deep sadness when she died. Then, he scribbled his address on a piece of paper and asked me to let him know someday how I was doing. This chance episode was one of the dearest moments in that long, dark time.

Friends often feel they have to cheer you up in sad times, but I think that grief has a lot to teach us and that getting on with our lives can begin only once the deep sadness is dealt with physically. Here is a way to let your body own and allow deep feelings of grief. —V.L.

What You Need

- One hour each day
- *A Grief Observed* by C. S. Lewis

What You Do

For one hour each day, for as many days as it feels necessary, take the time to be completely alone. Sit or lie down comfortably and let whatever you feel rise up into your body from feet to head. Try to allow your body to completely feel your grief, no matter how bad it gets.

Take deep, cleansing breaths whenever you need to, and stay in your experience as best you can. Give your mind something to do. Ask yourself, "What is the sensation I am feeling? Where does it hurt? How hot am I getting? How fast am I breathing?" If it helps, draw or write to express what you feel, holding nothing back.

During this period of grieving, avoid distractions, tedious people, shopping, drinking, and all other diversions that take you away from your feelings. It takes some time and some courage to grieve, but we are built to take it and we can survive deep grief and grow from it, if we honor ourselves and go slowly, one day at a time. It is important to remember that others are grieving, too. This is an excellent time to let the words of others who have grieved speak to you. Read C. S. Lewis's *A Grief Observed* and poems like this one.

A Wail Sighting off Kehoe Beach

The great heavy glass of the ocean
that falls to its knees in obeisance
to the land, then is yanked back home
in foam by the ankles, cannot
contain my grief.
Each black wave like loam curled back by the plough,
fritters its top away in lace as its power
tips and dives, yet I plunge more deeply.
Stink of the sea's detritus—the boas
of sea kelp decay; the crabs
like books of sodden cardboard matches dried—
all covered with busy flies—are not more sorry than I.

Blue ocean—blue sky.
Timpani of wave thunder, and snare
of pebbles and expended waves, and the sigh
of the last before the silent silk wipes
a mirror in the sand and leaves,
—let me cry.

—James McColley Eilers

The Death of a Parent

A man's dying is more the survivors' affair than his own.
—Thomas Mann

Before the father of my dear friend Sharon Swinyard died, he had started to play his violin again. One day, driving home from the doctor, he turned to Sharon and said, "I'm old now, aren't I?"

Active until the age of ninety-two, he had never stopped to think about his age until that moment. When he died, his daughter decided to let him lie in his bed while she gathered her sister, her mother, and her closest friends around his deathbed. We lit candles, arranged a vase of stargazer lilies, and kept a vigil for hours, recalling memories of him as they came to mind. Since I loved and respected this man, I was left with the feeling that I had shared something very intimate and profound with him and his family, a feeling I retain to this day.

There is no tie more dearly felt than the one between parent and child. Suddenly, without a parent as buffer, we are forced to confront our own mortality. The one who has kept us from painful things can no longer make it all right for us. We are all there is. The sense of grief and abandonment that can accompany the death of a parent is profound. The loving presence of friends can make the sadness more bearable and weave a once-in-a-lifetime memory. —V.L.

What You Need

- The family and close friends of the deceased
- A place to gather, preferably a home of one of the deceased's children
- A remembrance table
- A candle
- Your parent's favorite meal
- An eloquent song or reading

What You Do

If you are fortunate enough to be with your parent at the time of death, ask any medical professionals to give you time alone with your parent. No matter how kind they may be, unless you make this request they will follow protocol, not your needs. If possible, gather the key people in your life and keep a vigil at the bedside. Just breathe deeply and sit with the body. Being present as the soul departs the body is an incredible privilege. Stay with your parent as long as you can.

Later, set a time to gather immediate family and close friends in your home or in the home of one of your siblings. Have pictures, favorite objects, and other memorabilia displayed on a remembrance table so everyone can see and handle them. Items on the table may include a musical instrument or favorite sheet music, a wedding photo, a report card, a favorite baseball mitt, or sand from a beach visited on a memorable vacation.

Share your parent's favorite meal together, then move to a comfortable room, sit calmly, light a remembrance candle, and gather for a moment of silent reflection. After this time together feels complete, share a meaningful song or reading with the group, such as this one.

Death Is Nothing at All

I have only slipped away into the next room. I am I, and you are you. Whatever we were to each other, that we still are. Call me by my old familiar name, speak to me in the easy way that you always used. Put no difference in your tone, wear no forced air of solemnity or sorrow. Laugh as we always laughed at the little jokes we enjoyed together. Play, smile, think of me, pray for me. Let my name be ever the household word that it always was, let it be spoken without effort, without the trace of a shadow on it. Life means all that it ever meant. It is the same as it ever was; there is unbroken continuity. Why should I be out of mind because I am out of sight? I am waiting for you for an interval somewhere very near, just around the corner. All is well.

—Henry Scott Holland

Ask each person to recall a memory that has special meaning for her. It is good to include humorous anecdotes to lighten the tone and encourage conversation. Thank those present for the many ways they contributed to the life of the parent, and join hands, closing with these words: "We honor the life of our loved one and will treasure him always in our hearts and in our minds."

If the death follows a long period of suffering, acknowledge the role grown children played in the caretaking and acknowledge the end of that difficult passage, saying, "I release you as you release me; we are free to go forward in love and light."

A Ritual After a Death

Life is a great surprise. I do not see why death should not be an even greater one.

—Vladimir Nabokov

A very dear member of my family, my uncle Bush, lived alone until the age of ninety-one. No one was with him the night he died in his sleep. At first, I felt very sad because I didn't have the chance to comfort him and to say goodbye, yet I know that dying peacefully in his home was exactly what he would have wanted. Still, I wanted so badly to do something.

In Tibetan thinking, the moment of death is important, but even more so are the next seven weeks. After death, the deceased is thought to pass through the "bardo of becoming," a process in which he is challenged to move to higher and higher levels of consciousness. If he has enough support and is able to resist being drawn back into a physical body, he has the opportunity to realize complete enlightenment. Those of us who are living influence this passage by certain breathing practices and by holding good thoughts of the deceased for the seven weeks (forty-nine days) after death. Using the breath, Tibetan monks spend years practicing rituals for the dead.

Whether or not you believe in the bardo or reincarnation, what a wonderful tribute to someone you love to light a candle and simply breathe for him as you hold him in mind for forty-nine days. Whether he is helped you may not know, but you most certainly will be. —V.L.

What You Need

- A calendar
- Two boxes of birthday candles or a single votive candle
- A small candleholder
- Matches

What You Do

Mark on your calendar the day that is forty-nine days from the date of death. Light one small candle each day until you have reached the forty-ninth day. Some easy times to remember are at dinner or just before bed.

As you light the candle, fill your mind with positive thoughts of the person. Breathe in anything that may be unfinished or negative in the life of the deceased, and breathe out feelings of joy and release.

Honoring a Rich Life

When I am dead, I hope it may be said: "His sins were scarlet, but his books were read."

—Hilaire Belloc

I have been privileged to know two fine men whose funerals were truly celebrations of their lives. One was a doctor who originally wanted to be a concert violinist, the other, a distinguished judge who set new standards in our country for the education of judges. In both cases, the daughters of these men created remembrance tables displaying artifacts from their fathers' lives. The tables were rich with items of personal humor and symbols of the many contributions the men had made to the world.

Some of the items included a treatise on the education of judges, a much-loved fishing hat, and an unstrung violin bow. At each funeral, the items were a way for those present to relate to one another and compare notes on the many interesting aspects of the deceased's life. Wonderful memories came forth, as well as many warm smiles of recognition.

When a good life comes to an end, it is important to celebrate all of it, rather than dwelling on the circumstances of the person's final months, often a time of illness and sadness. In collecting the items, those grieving experience their deep feelings through the ritual handling of items hearkening to red-letter days of the past, familiar tastes and smells, and family high points of all kinds. —V.L.

What You Need

- An attractive table with a vase of flowers
- Special objects from the life of the loved one who has died
- A camera

What You Do

The day before the funeral or memorial service, arrange a table in the home or place where the group will gather after the service, labeling and displaying carefully selected items from the life of the deceased. Ask each person to be certain to visit the table, and station a knowledgeable family member at its side to interpret the items and answer questions. Be sure to photograph the collection before it is dispersed among relatives.

The Anniversary of a Death

A thief stole my precious jewels
in the black ink of night—
without a sound, gone forever,
diamonds without equal.
                    —Virginia Lang

Every year around the anniversary of my parents' deaths, I go through an emotional spin cycle. In March 1992, my mother died suddenly; six weeks later, my father followed her—both without warning. Now, when March rolls around, if I don't mentally prepare for it, I get knocked over by a wave of emotion. I had thought the grief I felt over the death of my mother and father would eventually play out like a hurricane downgraded to occasional showers; but instead, it seems to hit me again and again.

For many months after my parents died, I cut three Joseph's coat roses from my garden and made a small memorial to them every Thursday (the day I clean the house). One rose was for my mother, one was for my father, and the third rose was for a close friend killed in a skiing accident in New Zealand some years ago. This small gesture and its weekly continuity brought me great comfort and helped soften the suddenness and shock of all three deaths. —V.L.

What You Need

- A calendar
- A photo of the loved one who has died
- A flower and vase

What You Do

Mark the date of a significant death on your calendar well in advance. When the anniversary draws near, take out a picture of the person and place a small vase with a beautiful flower near it.

You may want to do this for just the day of the anniversary or for a longer period. If you like, add a small votive candle as well. When I was keeping up the ritual, I particularly liked searching for just the right rose, reflecting on each person's personality as I made my choice. Be kind to yourself and take time for personal reflection and solitude as the date approaches.

A Tragic Death

The agony is over. Hold on to the threads of light
go through the inky tunnel of night
pulled through darkness into light.

—Louise Nayer

One day, my husband and I got a call from our friend Laura. "I have AIDS," she said from a telephone at San Francisco General Hospital. Just two days before, I sat with her in a cafe while she told me of plans to go to Europe with her new love, Michael.

Soon after the diagnosis, Michael moved in with Laura, and he cared for her for the next two and a half years until her death. She was the only woman on the AIDS ward at that time, and there was still a lot of fear surrounding AIDS and how it spread. She was fortunate, though, to not be cut off from her family, who, after the initial shock, rallied to her bedside. In addition to her loving partner, Laura had many friends who visited her regularly.

Her spirit—which kept everyone so inspired for so long—prevailed even in death. Michael quickly got together an impromptu ceremony attended by everyone invited. Fifty people crowded into their living room the Wednesday after her death. Friends and family grieve in their own, often private, ways, but this was a moving ceremony that gave both groups of people a chance to be together and the opportunity to see more of Laura's life, even in death. —L.N.

What You Need

- A remembrance table
- The favorite music of the deceased
- Friends and family
- Poetry or other words about the person who has died
- A blank book in which people can write their thoughts, feelings, and memories, to be given to a loved one as a keepsake
- Potluck dishes provided by friends

What You Do

Create a remembrance table to express the loved one's life, including pictures from childhood to the present, favorite things like sand from a beach, childhood treasures, favorite books, creative projects, awards, and honors with family and friends so that many of the pieces of the person's life are intertwined. This also creates unity and new friendships among those who loved the person who has died.

Play the person's favorite music as people enter. Ask one person to serve as a guide for the evening and to give everyone a chance to talk through words, poetry, and song. Encourage people to speak about the deceased and to share precious memories with one another. Also encourage them to write a passage in the keepsake book.

Hopefully, family members and friends will talk and eat together, sharing phone numbers and keeping in touch, offering one another support. Let hugs abound and tears flow.

Holidays

As adults looking back on our lives, most of us remember holidays best of all, the pauses between work and school, the scents, the warm-oven smells, the ancient prayers and silent moments in places of worship, and the gatherings of relatives and friends.

In this section, we offer versions of time-honored and ancient celebrations, as well as cross-cultural and nontraditional holidays for families and single people.

Though many of us no longer live in direct contact with the earth, we still long to be in harmony with its rhythms and seasons and to take time to welcome the sacred parts of life into our hearts.

New Year's Eve

Follow the passages
Follow the hidden rooms
Life goes on from moon to moon.
—Louise Nayer

People follow many calendars throughout the world. But the one we're familiar with, the Gregorian calendar, designates January 1 as the first day of the year.

Janus (whose name is the root of January) is a Roman god portrayed with two faces. One face looks back toward the old year, and the other looks toward the new year. In his right hand, Janus holds a key that can close the door of the old year and open the door of the new year. On January 1, many of us also feel the need to close doors on what has gone before and think about what is to come.

New Year's Eve parties can be exciting—the glitter, the glitz, the ball dropping on Times Square. If you are with one you love, even better. But for many people, there is little depth of feeling in marking the new year. The only changes become simple ones—buying a new calendar or changing the date on a check. Here are two rituals that can be done on New Year's Eve to add meaning to the new year.

What You Need

- Close friends or family members who will stick with you throughout the year
- Pens and paper
- A hat
- Potluck dishes provided by everyone

What You Do

Ask each friend and family member to write down one change he would like to make in his life: "I would like to accept my mother this year for all she is and let go of past hurts." "I want to stop fighting with my teenage son." "I would like to get in shape and go on my first mountain climbing expedition." Sign your name to it.

After everyone has written something, put all changes in a hat. Have each person choose a slip of paper out of the hat and agree to be a coach for the person whose change they pick. The coach should check in at least once a month to help that person achieve his goal. The coach needs to do some research. "How can I help so-and-so accept her mother? Are there books that might help?" "In what way can I help this person get in shape? Are there inexpensive gyms nearby? A particularly good tape to buy?"

When everyone is matched up with a coach, agree that the group will meet at the same time next year. Emphasize that trying your best is most important and that results might vary. End the evening by saying, "We support one another as we work toward our goals for the new year." The following poem can also be read to end the evening.

> The shape of courage
> is round as your eyes,
> and sees to summits, lacy clouds, other worlds.
> The sound of courage is deep
> as a conch through a tunnel,
> pitch dark and light.
> The feel of courage is slippery,
> delicate as a thousand wings.
> The heart of courage is small
> as a finger
> the blood circulating
> in small spaces.
> always there
> like the air
>
> —Louise Nayer

Children's New Year

*My life turns like a spinning top, I am dancing in a dress
of ribbons. What are my colors? Where do I stop? What
will I be tomorrow?*

—Louise Nayer

New Year's Eve can be abstract for children because they measure
time by the school year and not by the Gregorian calendar. Explain
to them why we use this system to measure time and why New
Year's Eve marks a new beginning for everyone.

What You Need

- A quiet time on New Year's Eve or New Year's Day
- Pieces of different-colored ribbons
- A dowel or long stick

What You Do

Ask your child to pick aspects of her life that are important to her
and that she wants to weave into the year to come. Let her pick a
color that represents her desires—for instance, red for strength to
do her best in sports or green for courage to make new friends.
Help her wrap a ribbon around part of the dowel or stick. Add other
pieces of colored ribbon to be tied around the stick to represent
other desires until you have a multicolored stick. Hang it where
your child will see it every day. She does not need to tell anyone
of her wishes or desires.

Annual Family Time Capsule

Every instant of time is a pinprick of eternity.
—Marcus Aurelius Antoninus

My new friends Peter and Peggy Federico told me that every year for more than twenty years, their family has kept a time capsule to remember the highlights of the year gone by. On the last day of December, each child takes a large index card and writes the answers to these questions.

How old are you now?
How tall are you now?
What grade are you in?
Who are your favorite friends?
What is your favorite song?
What was your favorite movie this year?
Who do you most admire?
What is your favorite color?
What was your best moment? Worst moment?
What was your biggest surprise?
What are your hopes for next year?

All the answers are kept in a large water-tight container and read the next year on New Year's Eve. This has become a treasured family tradition in the Federico family and an excellent record of the children's growth. —V.L.

What You Need

- A list of questions
- Index cards and pens
- A large container

What You Do

Develop your own list of questions or borrow this one and, on December 31, ask each family member to complete the questions on an index card. They need not share their responses with one another. Put the responses in the time capsule container to be read the following New Year's Eve.

Celebrating the New Year with a Chinese Tradition

Words on a red cloth
Speak the hopes for coming days
Beckoning within.
                              —Virginia Lang

My daughter's name, YuWen, means "abundance and literature" or "rich culture," depending on your interpretation of the Chinese characters. In our family, we are learning to observe some time-honored Chinese traditions and to respect YuWen's rich heritage.

I particularly like the way Chinese families welcome the New Year—by visiting family, preparing ritual foods, and abstaining from work on days held sacred. Families write words of hope for good luck, good health, and prosperity on red cloths. They then hang them upside down on their front doors to indicate that the virtues or wishes they express will soon arrive in the homes. —V.L.

What You Need

- A gold marker
- A red cloth

What You Do

Think of your good wishes and hopes for the year ahead. They may be hopes for yourself, your family, or the world. Some examples are: "We hope to travel someplace special this year," "We hope Grandmother will enjoy good health this year," "We hope the world will be at peace this year."

Ask each person in the household to write their hopes in gold on the red cloth without judging themselves. You may prefer to write the expressions of hope on small pieces of fabric and sew those pieces onto the larger cloth. Hang the cloth upside down on the front door. Save the red cloth from each year as a family tradition.

Valentine's Day without a Valentine

Were beauty under twenty locks kept past
Yet love breaks through and picks them all at last.
—William Shakespeare

The trouble with holidays that celebrate the wonderful times in our lives is that they can also painfully underscore the absence of such times. Many of us have experienced a Valentine's Day when there has been little romance or passion, or one in which our love for another was unrequited. Unfortunately, there are no magic potions for matters of the heart, but there is an antidote to spending Valentine's Day in a funk.

What You Need

- A hospital or nursing home
- Red carnations or roses
- A person living alone, perhaps a student away at college, a soldier in the military, or an elder member of the family
- A handmade card

What You Do

Become the secret Valentine for someone else. Here are some simple ways.

Go to a hospital or nursing home near you with a bunch of red carnations. Tie onto each carnation a handwritten note, "Happy Valentine's Day from a secret admirer." Place one on each doorstep or mailbox, or give to the staff to hand out at dinner time. Hospitals have chart slots on the doors that make delivery easy. Taking a child along will make this especially fun.

If you know someone who is alone or far from home this year, create a special card with a timeless sentiment like the one below from the Song of Solomon. Sign it simply, "From a secret admirer." The recipient is sure to be intrigued and spend pleasant hours of happy imaginings!

> I am my lover's and he desires me.
> Come, my darling,
> let us go out into the fields
> and spend the night in villages.
> Let us wake early and go to the vineyards
> and see if the vine is in blossom,
> if the new grape bud is open
> and the pomegranates in bloom.
> There I will give you my love.
> The mandrakes will spray aroma

and over our door will be precious fruit,
new and old,
which I have saved for you, my darling.
        —The Song of Solomon 7:10–13

The Single Person's Valentine's Day

Each of us is an artist
Whose task is to shape life
Into some semblance of the pattern
We dream about.
                —*Arthur Graham*

Louise and I have a mutual friend, Jim Eilers, who is a gifted poet
and artist. He is also YuWen's godfather. As a single man, he often
dreads conventional holidays because they leave little room for his
perceptions of life and his way of knowing and feeling. Valentine's
Day can be especially rough for him.

When I asked him what he does for Valentine's Day, he said,
"On Valentine's Day, rather than being with someone I love, I do
what I love: I write!" While writing may not work for everyone, each
of us has a love, something that completely engages us, that trans-
ports us to another place in ourselves and awakens feelings of
self-love and self-worth. —V.L.

What You Need

- Time alone
- A place to pursue your love
- Andrea Marcovicci's beautiful vocal work "New Words" or
  similar beautiful music

What You Do

Let yourself be free of societal messages about love and simply be alone in a comfortable place. Breathe deeply, listen to Andrea Marcovicci, and follow the calling of your heart as you write, paint, sculpt, work in wood, or do whatever pleases you. Offer your creation as a Valentine's Day gift of love for yourself or someone else who lives alone.

Rite of Spring

This morning the green fists of the peonies are getting ready to break my heart . . .

—*Mary Oliver*

Spring explodes in Pennsylvania. It comes with an urgency and a will that is unstoppable. Ready or not, it spews forth armloads of brilliant forsythia, then scarlet azaleas, lavender rhododendrons, milky-white dogwood, and deep-grape Siberian irises.

In springtime, life pours from the earth without our having to do anything. It is a wonderful time to remember that we are not in control of nature, yet we are part of it. We deserve to be here just as much as the trees and flowers, not dominating the natural world but in a state of conscious participation with it. —V.L.

What You Need

- A place of privacy outdoors
- One of your favorite poems about nature

What You Do

Find a comfortable spot to lie face down on the ground. Let your body fully relax as it blends with the earth, and simply lie quietly, feeling the dynamic, life-giving power below you. A practice of the Q'ero Indians of Peru includes letting your navel come into direct contact with the ground to meld with the earth, considered the navel of creation. This simple, childlike posture can offer a profound experience of connection and peace. Stay as long as you like and breathe deeply.

Just before bed, read one of your favorite poems about our connection to nature. The words will help you sleep well and savor the magnificent gift that is spring.

Memorial Day

They shall beat their swords into plowshares, and their spears into pruning hooks: nation shall not lift up sword against nation, neither shall they learn war anymore.

—Isaiah 2:4

The theologian Matthew Fox says, "War is man's imagination gone mad without the balance of his compassion." Throughout the course of history, across cultures, we have defaulted to war when fear of "the other" has closed our hearts to our shared humanity, when our imagination has gone mad.

On a day set aside to remember men and women who fought for their countries, how do we honor them, while moving beyond war as a means of resolving conflict? Perhaps the mad side of our imagination needs a different way to express itself.

What You Need

- One hour alone
- A pencil and paper

What You Do

Write down the names of people you admire in history who died for an idea. They may be world leaders like Mahatma Gandhi or Martin Luther King Jr. or they may be friends or family members who fought in a war. Explore what you admire about them: What message of their lives is still important today?

Consider what you might do to further their work toward world peace. Here is a list of some possible short-term actions to start your thinking process.

- Examine the violence in yourself.
- Make peace with someone with whom you are "at war."
- Donate to Doctors Without Borders, the Red Cross, or another international relief agency.
- Write letters of support for Amnesty International.
- Help support a refugee family with your time, money, or professional expertise.
- Gather your family in a circle, light a candle for peace, and observe a moment of silence at your annual Memorial Day picnic.

Fourth of July

Man's capacity for justice makes democracy possible; but man's inclination to injustice makes democracy necessary.
—Reinhold Niebuhr

One Fourth of July, we took our daughter, YuWen, to her first fireworks at Penn's Landing in Philadelphia. As I stood in the shadow of Independence Hall with my Chinese child, watching a celebration of American freedom, tears came to my eyes as I thought of the delicious ironies—here she was in the city of my birth, free to be and to do whatever she likes, marking this freedom with firecrackers invented in China.

My mind drifted to a day when, from this same landing, my grandmother's sister, Anna, was forced to set sail for her native Ireland. She loved America and wanted to stay but was not a citizen and had to leave because she was engaged. Boarding the ship brokenhearted, she grew so ill on the passage home that she died in Ireland on her wedding day. As an American citizen, my daughter, whose full name is Anna YuWen, will have the freedom that her namesake, Anna Purser, did not.

On a day of great festivity, full of family picnics and sparklers, it is important that we, who live in a country that promises tolerance and equality, keep our awareness and gratitude for the gift of citizenship alive. May this holiday inspire us to work harder for justice for everyone in our country and in the world. —V.L.

What You Need

- A group of family or friends
- Four sparklers

What You Do

When it is very dark, gather the group in a circle. Choose four people to light freedom sparklers.

The first person should say, "We light this flame as grateful citizens of a free nation."

The second should say, "We light this flame for all the peoples of the world who do not live in freedom."

The third person, a veteran if possible, should say, "We light this flame for all who have given their lives for freedom and justice."

The fourth person should then say, "We light this flame as a symbol of hope for greater social justice in our country and freedom in the world."

If you know a new citizen or someone in the process of becoming one, invite him to join you. Light a fifth sparkler in his honor, with the words, "We salute you in your commitment to become a citizen of this country." Be sure to include older members of the family in this celebration, especially if there are any veterans. If possible, ask a veteran to read this poem.

In Flanders Fields

In Flanders fields the poppies blow
Between the crosses, row on row,
That mark our place; and in the sky
The larks, still bravely singing, fly
Scarce heard amid the guns below.
We are the Dead, short days ago
We lived, felt dawn, saw sunset glow,
Loved and were loved, and now we lie,
In Flanders fields.
Take up our quarrel with the foe:
To you from failing hands we throw
The torch; be yours to hold it high.
If ye break faith with us who die

We shall not sleep, though poppies grow
In Flanders fields.

—John McCrae

When the reader finishes, ask each person to observe a moment of silence to think about what it means to "break faith" with those who died for freedom.

Harvest Moon Festival

She opens her window
To the autumn moon's light.
She puts out the candle
And slips off her silken skirt.
Softly she smiles
Within the curtains of her bed.
She raises her body—
An orchid fragrance spreads.

—Anonymous

One of the most festive occasions in China is the Harvest Moon Festival. It celebrates the reunion of the Moon Goddess, who lives in the moon, with her husband, who lives in the sun. She has been banished to the moon because she stole the peach of immortality from her husband. One night a year, the night of the first full moon of autumn, she is permitted to join him.

In China, families dress in colorful costumes for this occasion and hold elaborate celebrations. An actor dressed as the Moon Goddess performs a ritual dance under the brilliant moon, and all beings, living and dead, connect through the moon.

In all cultures and times, the moon has always held a fascination for us. It is an intriguing thought that no matter where we are on earth, we can communicate with kindred spirits through the golden light of the harvest moon.

What You Need

* A group of friends or family
* The first full moon of autumn
* Moon cakes and jasmine tea

What You Do

Go outdoors and look at the moon together, thinking of all those living and dead who have gazed or have yet to gaze at the timeless moon. Send a silent message to someone far away, to be transmitted by the moon.

If you have young children, read aloud the beautiful children's book *The Moon Lady* by Amy Tan. A dancer in the family may choose to dress up and dance the part of the Moon Goddess as the story is read.

Share moon cakes and tea. You can buy moon cakes at a Chinese market during this time of year—or you can bake a simple moon-shaped cookie of your own.

Thanksgiving for a Couple

Do you carrot all for me?
My heart beets for you,
With your turnip nose
And your radish face,
You are a peach.
If we cantaloupe,
Lettuce marry;
Weed make a swell pear.
                    —Anonymous

The first Thanksgiving my husband and I shared was indeed memorable. We were with a group of twenty-two people, all of whom were strangers to one another. We sat on the floor and the Thanksgiving meal was served Tom Jones–style: We fed one another, laughing at the simple pleasure that this brought to the celebration, and all awkwardness began to disappear. The group quickly dispensed with small talk, giving itself over to real merriment and gratitude for the food and for one another.

When a bride and groom feed each other the first piece of wedding cake, each is symbolically offering to nurture the other. Thanksgiving is a wonderful time for two people to renew their commitment to "feed" each other through this joyful and very intimate rite of gratitude. —V.L.

What You Need

- A low table and pillows
- Lots of napkins
- A festive meal
- Finger bowls with fresh lemon slices

What You Do

Get comfortable on the pillows, join hands, and say your holiday blessing. Eat the Thanksgiving meal Tom Jones–style, each person feeding the other with hands only, using napkins and dipping in lemon finger bowls as needed.

Thanksgiving with Children

Be not forgetful to entertain strangers: for thereby some have entertained angels unawares.

—Hebrews 13:2

The spirit of Thanksgiving can be difficult for children to understand. Do little children have any real connection with pilgrims and the *Mayflower* or the significance of these people sharing a meal with Native Americans?

It may be that a living demonstration is needed, with someone who is unknown joining the family table and expanding the meaning of family and inclusion.

What You Need

- The name of someone who may not have local relatives, someone living alone, a single-parent family, or a family with few resources
- An invitation
- Craft supplies for handmade place mats and place cards

What You Do

Have your child write out an invitation asking the chosen person or family to join you and your family for Thanksgiving. Deliver the invitation by hand and be sure to offer transportation to and from the gathering.

Make a festive place mat and place card for each person, taking care to correctly spell the names of your invited guests. As the meal is served, ask the youngest reader to offer a family prayer or to read the following prayer.

Iroquois Thanksgiving Prayer

We return thanks to our mother, the earth
which sustains us . . .
to the wind, which moves the air that banishes disease . . .
to our grandfather Creator who has
protected his grandchildren and has given
to us his rain . . . to the sun that has looked
upon the earth with a beneficent eye.

Afterward, ask everyone to join hands and say, "We give thanks for this meal and the chance to share it together." Extend a warm message of welcome to the guests, and enjoy the gathering!

Hanukkah

Sometimes the whole sky turns into an otherworldly Hanukkah lamp, with the stars as its lights. I told my dreams to a rabbi and he said, "Love comes from the soul and souls radiate light."

—Isaac Bashevis Singer

Although my father is Jewish, our family did not celebrate Jewish holidays. It was only after my daughter Sarah attended the Jewish community center and announced, "We need to buy a Hanukkah menorah" that we began to celebrate the holiday. Many interfaith couples celebrate this festival, and there are many occasions when non-Jews are invited to the homes of Jewish people to share in this time and to think about how everyone can become free from oppression and persecution.

Hanukkah lasts eight days and is usually celebrated in December. It commemorates the struggle of the Jews against the Syrian-Greeks. After the Jews' victory, they returned to their city of Jerusalem to restore the partially destroyed Temple. At the Temple, the Jews found only one small cruse of oil to light the eternal light. By some miracle, the oil lasted for eight days, time enough to procure more oil. The light never went out. It was proclaimed a miracle, to be commemorated every year.

Though it is not a major holiday, Hanukkah is celebrated widely because of its proximity to Christmas and because of its message that all people should be free to worship in peace. —L.N.

What You Need

- Nine candles
- A Hanukkah menorah

- Friends or family
- Paper and pens
- Food made with oil, such as jelly doughnuts or potato latkes
- A dreidel
- Gelt (chocolate coins wrapped in gold foil—the gold represents light)

What You Do

At sundown, after dinner, use a helper candle to light the candle on the far-right side of the menorah. Most families say, either in Hebrew or in English, the prayer, "Blessed are You, Lord our God, King of the Universe, Who has sanctified us with His commandments and commanded us to kindle the light of Hanukkah."

Each night for the next seven nights, light one more candle, continuing to go from right to left. If you wish, place the Hanukkah menorah in the window for all to see.

On a big piece of paper, write out the word freedom. Ask everyone, including the children, to write, "I feel free when . . . I can work for freedom in the world by . . ."

Hang up the sheet of paper as a reminder of the work we need to do to create peace in the world. Eat the fried food and play dreidel with the kids.

Instructions for Playing Dreidel

The game dreidel began when Jews were forbidden to study the Torah, the Jewish Bible. Boys would study together secretly, and when they heard the footsteps of soldiers, they pulled out spinning tops and pretended to be playing games. Though children in the past carved their own wooden dreidels, now the toys can be bought in many stores. The dreidel has four sides, each one inscribed with the letter nun, gimmel, he, or shin, which mean together "A great miracle happened there."

All players are given an equal number of gelt, or they may use raisins, candies, or any objects they choose. To begin, each player takes five objects from her pile and puts them into a common pile. Then, everyone takes a turn spinning the dreidel. When the spin lands on nun, it means do nothing; on gimmel, take the common pile; on he, take half the common pile; and on shin, give half of the spinner's pile. When a player has nothing left to give, she is out of the game. The player who still has a pile when everyone else is out is the winner.

Day of the Dead

Death was not the natural end of life but one phase of an infinite cycle.

—*Octavio Paz*

The Mexican Day of the Dead is an ancient festival, transformed from the original celebration into one that coincides with a Christian holiday, All Hallows' Eve. Families visit gravesites, picnic on the grass, and place brightly colored flowers on the graves. It is a time to remember, to tell stories about the dead, and to feast.

In San Francisco's Mission District, you can buy small sugar skulls and dioramas filled with dancing skeletons. Sometimes people buy special bread filled with a plastic toy skeleton to offer to the dead.

Whether you are honoring a close friend, a relative, or anyone precious to you who has passed away, this ritual may help you reconnect with that person and with what touched you so deeply about his life.

Though the Mexican celebration is around Halloween, you can also remember a loved one each year on the anniversary of his death.

What You Need

- A small table
- A tablecloth
- A vase and brightly colored flowers
- Photographs of your loved one or other memorabilia such as pieces of clothing
- A small basket
- Festive music
- Your loved one's favorite food or a loaf of bread
- A candle
- Blank index cards and colored pens
- A photo album

What You Do

Before dinner on November 1 or on the anniversary of your loved one's death, set up a special table anywhere you choose. Make sure to involve children in the preparations. Cover the table with a colorful cloth. Place a vase with flowers in the center and arrange the photos and other keepsakes around the flowers. Place the small, empty basket near the flowers.

After dinner, play music. Dance, if you like! Put out a small portion of the deceased's favorite food. Turn the lights down in the room, light the candle, and say what you loved about the person. Afterward, write notes on the index cards and place them in the basket. You may continue to write notes over the next few days or as long as the special table is in place. Later, you can keep the messages in a photo album, along with photos of your loved one.

Winter Solstice

It is the darkest day of the year
when we fold into ourselves
like feathered birds
gazing at the inside
of a candle flame,
at the small sparks of humanity,
the place of light.

—Louise Nayer

The winter solstice is celebrated on the shortest day of the year, usually December 21. Long ago, people feared that the sunlight would not come back again. They began the tradition of burning yule logs to help bring back the light.

In celebrating the solstice, we celebrate the seasons of change and honor Mother Earth. Here are two rituals, one to be done with family and one to be done alone on the night of December 21 to remember the light that will come back and eventually turn the barren earth into fields of green.

What You Need

- Friends or family gathered together
- Log in a fireplace, if possible
- Candles with holders
- Music
- Cookies or cake with poppy or sesame seeds
- Hot cider

What You Do

If you have a fireplace, gather around and light a log. Turn out all the lights in the house and sit in darkness, asking everyone to think about the light and look into the fire. If you don't have a fireplace, everyone can look into the flame of a large candle. Ask even the children to be silent for a minute or two.

During this time of silence, ask everyone to think for a couple of minutes about what has happened this year and what is to come in the new year. Tell the children to focus on how they overcame problems and difficulties during the past year and how the adults will be there to help them fulfill their hopes and dreams for the new year.

Go around the room and ask everyone to offer a wish for the earth: "I hope the trees will get enough sunlight this year" or "I hope the birds return to Glen Park Canyon when spring comes."

Then, pass out small candles with holders. Ask one child to light his candle. Pass the light around from one person to the next. Put music on. After all the candles are lit, say, "Let our light shine inside us and outside us through the darkness of winter."

Blow out the candles, turn on the lights, and serve the cookies or cakes, their seeds symbolizing new life. Drink hot cider and decide to do something individually or together to replenish the earth in the next year.

After the children have gone to bed, the adults can stay up until midnight to more fully experience the darkness. Consider the words of the following prayer.

Zuni Prayer to the Sun

Who among men and all creatures
Could live without the Sun Father?
For his light brings day, warms and
gladdens the Earth Mother with rain,
Which flows forth the water we drink.

And that causes the flesh of the
Earth Mother to yield seeds abundantly.
—Zuni tribe

Heartfelt Christmas

I made the frame for you and painted it the color
blue, your favorite hue. I made the frame
especially for you and filled it with me,
smiling back at you.

—Louise Nayer

Christmas presents appear in stores the minute Thanksgiving ends, sometimes even before. We are bombarded with advertisements about expensive gifts that many of us can't afford and don't really want. Over the past fifteen years, as my family has struggled with our budget, Christmas has been especially difficult. Though we want to continue giving our children and our friends' children one or two presents that they really want, we have now modified Christmas so that we make presents for the adults.

It's also important to remember that many people simply cannot afford expensive items and that making gifts is an honorable and more memorable solution to the blues resulting from overspending. This year in my family, we gave photos to one another. In contrast to gifts stuffed in drawers or never worn, the photos are proudly displayed on our bookshelf and the bookshelves of our friends and family. —L.N.

What You Need

- Many ideas for simple-to-make gifts
- Creative ways of giving of yourself

What You Do

Because making gifts takes a lot more time than shopping, pick one day each weekend starting in October to create your gifts. Two hours are sufficient each weekend and must be planned on the calendar.
Here are some gift ideas.

- Frame photographs. You can also paint the frame and decorate it by gluing seashells, buttons, ribbons, and glitter on it. Frame photos of friends or family. Start early with taking the photos.
- Do what you do best. I write poetry, so I have often given gifts of my poems printed on thick cream-colored paper and framed. My husband loves to sculpt. Last year, he sculpted white porcelain Christmas tree ornaments. My daughters both like to make jewelry and have made many presents of necklaces and earrings.
- Prepare food. Everyone loves to get a tin of homemade cookies or a loaf of homemade bread. These can be cooked early in the season and kept frozen, then placed in a decorative tin.
- On a handmade card, offer to perform a service, such as a neck massage, a day of cleaning and painting, or a lunch out.
- For some people who might not want gifts, offer to do community service in honor of that person, helping in a soup kitchen, reading stories to seriously ill children, or organizing a neighborhood park cleanup. All ages can be involved.

Acknowledgments

For their encouragement and support, I wish to thank Margaret Bauer; Mary Rowse; George Lang; the late Frederick Lang; Heather Michelson; Ellen and Mark Borenstein; Peter and Nick Borenstein; Emily Defraites; Sharon Swinyard; David Sutton; Ray Ling Hou Chang; Ken Petron; Panna Flower; Diana Condon; Nitza Agam; Mitani D'Antien; Americo Yabar; Susan Eisenberg; Gail Grimes; Claude Whitmyer; Rosario Fernandez; Ann Mayer Heselwood; Carole Garland; Jim Eilers; Judy Maselli; Sarah Patten; Laura Patten; Morgan Green; Louise Bennett; Rita Rine; Aldona Watts; Myrna Chapman; Barbara Le Maire; Alexis Arrow; Peggy Luke; Judy McCarthy; Bill Pinder; the Kimmel, Maruska, Wellington, Federico, Martin, and Green families; and the staff of the Countryside Market of Swarthmore, Pennsylvania.

—V.L.

For their love and guidance, I first want to thank Jim, Sarah, and Laura Patten; my parents, Dorothy and Hank Nayer; also Anne Nayer and Lily McMenamin; Bonnie Patten and George Brencher; Janice Bressler; Josee Andrei; Bill Wallace; Jeri McGovern; the people at my Unitarian Universalist congregation, including Pat Post, John Marsh, Barbara Conahan, and Betsy Darr; Jim Eilers; Myrna Chapman; Barbara Le Maire; Aldona Watts; Dixie Morse; Spencer Michels; Alexis Arrow; Peggy Luke; Claire Thurston; Mimi Fried; Leslie Simon; Anita and Elizabeth Strong; Dr. Rong Rong Zheng; YuWen Michelson Lang; Lynn Levy; Cathy DeRosas and Penny Speckter; Nina Lathrop; Helen Grossman; and in memory of Reverend and Mrs. Daubert.

—L.N.

We are grateful to Mary Benard and Marshall Hawkins, our editors at Skinner House, for their belief in the book; and special thanks to Amber Gutebier.